The Secret Language of Intimacy

•••••••••••••••••

Robert G. Lee

•••••••••••••••••

The Secret Language of Intimacy

· · · · · · · · · · · ·

Releasing the Hidden Power in Couple Relationships

A GestaltPress Book

Published and distributed by
Routledge, Taylor & Francis Group
New York

Copyright 2008 by: The GestaltPress
127 Abby Court
Santa Cruz, CA 95062

and   165 Route 6A
Orleans, MA 02653

Email: gestaltpress@aol.com, gestaltpress@comcast.net

Distributed by: Routledge, Taylor & Francis Group
711 Third Avenue
New York, NY 10017

Library of Congress Cataloging-in-Publishing Data
1. couples, 2. shame, 3. intimacy, 4. Gestalt therapy,
5. counseling, 6. Robert Gerald Lee

ISBN 978-0-145-99214-5

For my wife Debbie
and for my children and step-children,
and their families
Chris, Dina, Pam, Phyllis,
Steve and Julia, Schuyler,
Jasmine, David and Solon

Contents

◆◆◆◆◆◆◆

Part 1 - The Secret Language of Intimacy Workshop

Robert G. Lee

Part 2 – Contributors' Essays

Preface

●●●●●●●●●●●●●●●●●●

Couples have always had a special place in my heart. Said in a larger context, *I believe in couples*. When couple relationships work well, the people within them gain a multifaceted power that permeates their lives, literally keeping them energetically alive and healthy.

This is not a romantic fantasy, this reality has long been documented by research. For example, Glen and Weaver (1981) concluded from their study that "for most adults happiness depends upon having a good marriage more than anything else" (p. 166). A number of studies have reported that close, confiding, intimate relationships have been found to be "powerful mediators" between severe life events and the onset of a psychiatric disorder (e.g., Brown et al., 1978) or depression, in particular (Costello, 1982; Roy, 1981; Solomon & Bromet, 1982). Others have concluded that even without a precipitating event, the presence of a close relationship is important for emotional health (Aneschenel & Stone, 1982; Thoits, 1982). The safety and love of a close relationship is unparalleled in its potential for providing an atmosphere to process our experience in the world and to form new conceptualizations of self and other as our lives evolve.

My own research (Lee, 1994) found that in couples, in which both partners experienced a high sense of *emotional safety*, partners not only liked being with each other, could tell each other their deepest feelings and concerns, thought of each other as best friends, were affectionate with each other, and had great sex, they also reported having good problem solving skills, so that they could better deal collectively and individually with the challenges that life brought them. Accordingly, it is not surprising that a study on people in the later stages of their lives found that the happiest and healthiest subjects were those who had been involved in close relationships. (Lowenthal & Haven, 1968)

The other side of this reality has also been well documented. A lack of intimacy in couples has long been correlated with such personal difficulties as psychosomatic symptoms (Waring, 1980), non-psychotic emotional disorders (Brown & Harris, 1978; Hames & Waring, 1980; Renne, 1971; Waring et al., 1986), chronic illness and disability (Renne, 1971) and enmeshed family structures (Waring & Russell, 1980).

This is all in sync with what we have been learning more recently from neurobiological research—that we are wired for affective attunement (See Stern et al., 2003) and that relationship plays a primary role in the ongoing development of the brain (Siegel, 1999).

Perhaps Lowenthal and Weiss (1976), who studied intimacy over many years, best summed up the importance of couple intimacy:

The striving for interpersonal intimacy..., next to the dire necessities of life, is perhaps the basic human need... in the absence of overwhelming external challenge, most "average" men and women find the energy and motivation to live... satisfying lives only through one or more mutually supportive and intimate dyadic relation ships. (p. 11)

Thus, the rewards for helping couples find their way to the cohesiveness they seek are great.

This book has grown out of the powerful insights and discoveries that have emerged in the course of helping couples navigate the hidden morass that blocks their attempts to connect with each other. At one time that seemed to be such a frustrating and impenetrable task—*until I discovered there is a code and started to learn how to unravel the code.*

Let me bring you up to date on my journey of discovery. I had been a Gestalt couples' therapist for some thirteen years, with a solid foundation from the relational approach of the Gestalt Institute of Cleveland's Intimate Systems Program in 1980, when, in 1987, I picked up a book by Gershen Kaufman (1980) called *Shame: The Power of Caring.* My movement toward unlocking the hidden power in couple's interactions suddenly took an additional leap forward. Kaufman was writing about the phenomenon of shame in individuals. However, I recognized that this could be the hidden element with which my couple clients were struggling. Was this why some couples could handle unbelievably complicated differences between partners while others couldn't join to decide something as simple as in which bank they wanted to open a joint account?

I subsequently undertook a research study on the effects of shame in marital relationships (Lee, 1994), which revealed a host of crucial effects of this hidden dynamic in couple interactions. Kaufman became a valued consultant during that process.

In the course of this research I became interested in the connection between shame and Gestalt theory and discovered that Gestalt's prime focus was in fact the phenomenon of shame. Gestalt theorists such as Perls and Goodman had been writing largely about shame without mentioning it by name. In a 1995 article (Lee, 1995), I showed how Perls' concept of an "introject" (swallowing whole a way of being in the world that is not natural to the individual, e.g., "I should not be angry," which Perls proposed was the core of neurosis) was actually a form of shame. Coming to understand the heart of Gestalt theory in this way deepened my understanding of the field conditions which foster the development of shame oriented creative adjustments (including those labeled by Perls as "introjects," "projections," and "retroflections") as well as the power that fixes them in place.

In the process of learning more about Gestalt through the lens of shame, the lens of Gestalt in turn provided a clearer view of the phenomenon of shame. And subsequently, together with Gordon Wheeler, I co-edited and published *The Voice of Shame; Silence and Connection in Psychotherapy* (Lee & Wheeler, 1996), which from a Gestalt field perspective focused on how shame and belonging regulate the social field.

All this further informed my evolving understanding of the hidden elements in couples' dynamics. This growing knowledge brought new awarenesses when I sat with couples. I found myself changing. Over several years a new form emerged that

that I further adapted for working with a number of couples at one time, in an intensive group setting.

The Secret Language of Intimacy Workshop, Part I of this book, is an integration of my experience, research, and theoretical discoveries with respect to couples. It is the presentation of a workshop which I first developed and presented at the 3rd Annual Conference of the Association for the Advancement for Gestalt Therapy in 1998. Since then this workshop has been requested and presented in London, Sydney, Melbourne, Brisbane, Big Sur, Cleveland and other Australian and US locations. It has helped couples to transform experiences of misconnection and disillusionment into opportunities for greater intimacy and connection.

In true Gestalt fashion, I wanted to bring you a variety of practitioner experiences and viewpoints, as well as bring you a fuller sense of couples' experience. I have been fortunate to be able to enlist the talents of a group of leading practitioners from countries around the world, reflecting the cutting edge of Gestalt couples therapy in a number of different cultures. I am indebted to their brilliance and experience as well as the well thought out uniqueness of their perspectives.

The book opens, Part I (Chapters 1 through 5), with the presentation of "The Secret Language of Intimacy Workshop," describing not only how the hidden forces of shame and belonging regulate couple dynamics, but also how this workshop facilitates couples embracing these concepts, coming to appreciatively understand their relational connections anew, and discovering the hidden power that emanates from their yearnings. In Chapter 5, there are several vignettes of my working with volunteer couples at the end of Sec. Lang. of Int. workshops, more fully explicating and demonstrating how these variables fit together.

Part II starts with an exquisitely written piece, Chapter 6, "Being at the Contact Boundary with the Other: The Challenge of Every Couple," by Margherita Spagnuolo Lobb in Italy. Spagnuolo Lobb, a long time master trainer, therapist, and brilliantly refreshing presence on the international Gestalt scene, eloquently and compassionately captures the delicate nature of the universal human experience of intimately meeting another.

Next, in Chapter 7, "Work with Couples in Mexico from a Gestalt Approach," Marina Ayo Balandrazo & Enrique Mercadillo Madero bring us an account of the cultural dilemmas facing Mexican couples. Here we get a sharper sense of how the forces of shame and belonging can manifest in the environment for couples, lessons that have implications for other cultural situations as well. They generously share their comprehensive program that is based on appreciative understanding and supportive implementation in addressing couple's shame and belonging dynamics.

Ed and Barbara Lynch bring their extensive experience in training therapists and working with couples and families, from their USA university setting, in authoring Chapter 8, "Understanding the Complexity of Intimacy." Through their adept insights we not only gain a broader understanding of the components and complexity of couple intimacy but also are provided a greater sense of how family of origin history can contribute to the hidden taboos and knots that interfere with couple connection. They share with us a "projective" technique that they have used for twenty five years in working with both individuals and couples in helping people discover the relational patterns in their family of origin.

In Chapter 9, "The Secret Life of Us," Brian & Jenny O'Neill, long time leaders in Australian Gestalt as well as the international community, share with us their conceptualization of the couple as a "oneness," rather than two individuals. Viewing the couple from this perspective permits a clearer sense of how couple partners act together in ways that they themselves are unaware of. On one side, couples' troubled behavior may stem from a shared belief that connection and belonging are not possible in some manner; on the other side, couples may not be aware of the power of their spiritual or harmonious connection. Of equal importance is the O'Neills' generosity and sensitivity in sharing with us how they have used the experiences of their own relationship to understand and work with the clients they serve.

In the final chapter, Chapter 10, "Joint Constructions: On the Subject Matter of Gestalt Therapy, Exemplified by Gender-Specific Misunderstandings with Regard to Intimacy," we are treated to the compassionate understanding and brilliance of Frank Staemmler, from Germany. Long one of the most respected presences in the field of Gestalt, Staemmler gives us an acute understanding of the hidden gender differences in meaning making that can lie beneath troubled couple interactions. He shares a process he has developed to enable couple partners to transcend the boundaries of their own meaning making systems and to come to discover and explore the realm of joint meanings. As couple partners develop a mutual knowledge of and respect for their individual meanings, their intersubjective integration of these understandings transports them into a higher, relational level.

This is the book—rounded out with an Afterword.

As with my past writings, my hope is that this is not an end but part of a continuing dialogue in the field on the understandings and tools that help couples unlock the hidden power in their relationships, supporting them to realize the potential that drew them together. It is with these thoughts that I wish you the experience of pleasurable and profitable reading.

Robert G. Lee
2008, Newton, Massachusetts

References

Aneschenel, C. S., & Stone, J. D. (1982). Stress and depression: A test of the buffering model of social support. *Archives of General Psychiatry*, 39, 1392-1396.

Brown, G. W., & Harris, T. (1978). *Social Origins of Depression*. London: Tavistock.

Brown, G. W., Brolchain, M. D., & Harris, T. (1975). Social class and psychiatric disturbance among women in an urban population. *Sociology*, 9, 225-254.

Costello, C. G. (1982). Social factors associated with depression: A retrospective community sample. *Psychological Medicine*, 12, 329-340.

Glenn, N. D., & Weaver, C. N. (1981). The contribution of maritial happiness to global happiness. *Journal of Marriage and the Family, 43,* 161-168.

Hames, J., & Waring, E. M. (1980). Marital intimacy and non-psychotic emotional illness. *The Psychiatric Forum, 9,* 13-19.

Kaufman, G. (1980). *Shame: The Power of Caring.* Rochester VT: Shenckman.

Lee, R. G. (1995). Gestalt and shame: The foundation for a clearer understanding of field dynamics. *The British Gestalt Journal, 4*(1), 14-22.

Lee, R. G. (1994). The effect of internalized shame on marital intimacy. (Unpublished doctoral dissertation, Fielding Institute, Santa Barbara, CA.)

Lee, R. G., & Wheeler, G. (Eds.). (1996). *The Voice of Shame: Silence and Connection in Psychotherapy.* San Francisco: Jossey-Bass.

Lowenthal, M. F., & Haven, C. (1968). Interaction and adaptation: Intimacy as a critical variable. *American Sociological Review, 33*(1), 20-30.

Lowenthal, M. F., & Weiss, L. (1976). Intimacy and crises in adulthood. *The Consulting Psychologist, 6*(1), 10-15.

Renne, K. S. (1971). Health and marital experience in an urban population. *Journal of Marriage and the Family, 33,* 338-350.

Roy, A. (1981). Vulnerability factors and depression in men. *British Journal of Psychiatry, 138,* 75-77.

Solomon, Z., & Bromet, E. (1982). The role of social factors in affective disorder: An assessment of the vulnerability model of Brown and his colleagues. *Psychological Medicine, 12,* 123-130.

Thoits, P. A. (1982). Conceptual, methodological and theoretical problems in studying social support as a buffer against life stress. *Journal of Health and Social Behavior, 23,* 145-159.

Waring, E. M. (1980). Marital intimacy, psychosomatic symptoms, and cognitive therapy. *Psychosomatics, 21,* 596-601.

Waring, E. M., Patton, D., Neron, C. A., & Linker, W. (1986). Types of marital intimacy and prevalence of emotional illness. *Canadian Journal of Psychiatry, 31,* 720-726.

Waring, E. M., & Russell, L. (1980). Family structure, marital adjustment, and intimacy in patients referred to a consultation-liaison service. *General Hospital Psychiatry, 3,* 198-203.

Acknowledgments

•••••••••••

The ideas in this book are grounded in a respect for and awe of what it means to be in a committed intimate relationship. I will always be indebted to my initial trainers, Faith and Peter, from the Student Counseling Center at the State University of New York at Buffalo, who, as a teaching technique, generously afforded me and their other trainees an intimate view of their evolving relationship. They essentially put themselves in our hands at times of uncertainty and self doubt, conflict and anger, threat of personal loss, and joy and celebration. Their integrity, courageous ability to face into their own and each other's vulnerability, resilience, ability to enjoy themselves and each other, and their spiritual connection are still with me.

Similarly this book could not be possible without the relational foundation in working with couples and families that was given to me by two of my long time mentors, Sonia Nevis and Joseph Zinker. Over the course of a decade of training (late '70s to late '80s), in the forms of two major clinical programs, numerous workshops, and ongoing supervision from Sonia, I developed a sense of the importance of support, how to see a couple system, and how to hold and respond to couples in a balance manner.

The faculty of one of the above mentioned trainings (Gestalt Institute of Cleveland's Intimate Systems Program, 1980) bears additional mention, in particular Wes Jackson and Les Wyman.

I have already referred to my extensive debt to Gershen Kaufman in the Preface to this book. I can only add my appreciation for how his understanding of shame opened new theoretical possibilities for me with regard to both Gestalt theory, in general, and couple dynamics, in particular.

The ideas that support the Secret Language of Intimacy Workshop have been refined and clarified in the course of presenting this workshop at two Association for the Advancement of Gestalt Therapy Conferences (1998 & 2002) and in a number of other venues around the world, over the last nine years. I am deeply appreciative of Toni Gilligan, Steve Vinay Gunther, Rhonda Gibson Long, Nancy Lunney-Wheeler, Philip Oldfield, Brian and Jenny O'Neill, Gabe Phillips, Jane Puddy, Bronagh Starrs and the other members of Borealis, Claire Taubert, Maria Vogt, Jacqueline Wearn, Gordon Wheeler, and Greer White. These directors of institutes and training facilities around the world have continuously supported the development and dissemination of these ideas and of me through their warmth, hospitality, and enthusiasm.

A special thank-you goes to Tim Warneka for locating the image used on the front cover as well as for his skill and time in incorporating the image into an artistic, graceful cover design.

The couples who have attended my workshops and who I have seen in my practice have honored me with their trust and the intimacy of their lives. They have grounded and refined my ideas in the truth of their experience. Bearing witness to their yearning for connection, their courage and willingness to struggle and endure, and the unbelievable joy that comes with true intimacy has deeply moved me.

Two dear, close, treasured friends, Lee Geltman and Gordon Wheeler, who have been sounding boards and voices of support since my earliest explorations as an author, once again deserve particular acknowledgment and thanks. Not only did the work that I undertook with Gordon, exploring shame and belonging's regulation of the relational field, ground and illuminate my thinking and evolution as a theoretician, in addition it was Gordon who initially encouraged me to give voice to the concepts and methodologies which make up Part I of this book. Lee's willingness to continuously challenge me to refine and articulate my message, his attention to the rhythm and flow of my language, his creative suggestions, and his caring presence and friendship provided me with much needed energy and significantly honed the form and presentation of this book.

Most importantly, I want to thank my love, my partner and fellow voyager through this ongoing adventure of life, my wife Debbie. It is with her that I have learned the The Secrect Language of Intimacy from the inside out and have experienced first hand the unbelievable fulfillment and power that comes with a connective relationship.

Robert G. Lee

The Author

◆◆◆◆◆◆◆◆◆◆◆

Robert G. Lee, PhD, a psychologist in private practice in Cambridge, Massachusetts, USA, has written extensively and presented widely on shame and belonging as regulator processes of the relational field. He applies his intersubjective, constructivist insights to a wide range of clinical populations, including working with individuals, couples, families, children and adolescents, as well as to the topics of self process, development, field theory, ethics, culture, gender, and chronic illness. His research on couples and shame led to a deeper understanding of the hidden dynamics of the intimate couple. His article, "Gestalt and Shame: The foundation for a Clearer Understanding of Field Dynamics," won the 1995 Nevis Prize for Outstanding Contribution to Gestalt Therapy Theory. Robert is co-editor of *The Voice of Shame: Silence and Connection in Psychotherapy*. (Jossey-Bass, 1996). His recent collected work, *The Values of Conneciton: A Relational Approach to Ethics* (GestaltPress/The Analytic Press, 2004), explores the values of connection that emerge from the Gestalt model and how they provide an ethical basis for working and interacting with others, offering field solutions for modern problems. He is an editor of GestaltPress, a member of the faculty of the Gestalt Institute of Cleveland, and a visiting faculty member of Gestalt Training programs in Australia, Europe and the USA. Other interests in his life include dancing, snorkeling, and being with and enjoying his wife and their collective children.

The Contributors

••••••••••••••

Marina Ayo Balandrazo, MDH, is founder and co-director of the Unidad de Psicoterapia Asesoria y Desarrollo de Occidente A.C., a Gestalt institute in Guadalajara, México. A Gestalt therapist in private practice and teacher and trainer in a diverse variety of Mexican universities since 1990, she has specialized in working with and creating therapuetic programs for couples since 2000.

J. Edward Lynch, PhD & Barbara J. Lynch, PhD are professors in the Marriage & Family Therapy department in the graduate school of Health and Human Services at Southern CT State University. They have both been on the faculty for more that 25 years. Ed is the Department Chairperson while Barbara is the Program Director. They have co-authored the book "Principles & Practices of Structural Family Therapy" and numerous articles and chapters in various texts. Ed co-authored "Messengers of Healing," a book devoted to Family Constellations. Both Ed and Barbara are workshop facilitators throughout the United States and Europe. In addition to Marriage and Family Therapy, Ed specializes in Gestalt Therapy and Family Constellations. Barbara supplements her primary work with a specialty in couples' relationships and with clinical supervision for therapists working with couples. They live on the Long Island Sound shore with their therapy dog Madison, who works in the Family Clinic with children coming for supervised visits.

Enrique Mercadillo Madero, MDH, a Gestalt therapist in private since 1999 and a professor in a variety of diverse universities in México since 1996, lives and works in Monterrey. He is a partner of the Unidad de Psicoterapia Asesoria y Desarrollo de Occidente A.C in Monterrey and co-founded Human Processes, a consulting and Psychotherapy institution, in 2003. He has been working with couples since 2003.

Brian O'Neill BA, MAPS, a registered psychologist, is co-director of the Illawarra Gestalt Centre, in Australia and visiting faculty member of Gestalt Training programs in Australia, the USA and Europe. He is past President of the Association for Advancement of Gestalt Therapy (AAGT), founding editor of the Gestalt Therapy Forum (New York), a board member of Gestalt Global, and on the editorial boards of the Gestalt Review and Studies in Gestalt. He is a Senior Fellow in Mental Health (University of Wollongong), and a member of the College of Counseling Psychologists (Australian Psychological Society). He has worked in the drug and alcohol field, mental health services and HIV/AIDS and more recently as Deputy State Director with Department of Veterans Affairs working with couples in the context of war and PTSD. He is currently the regional manager for Relationships Australia, for the Illawarra Region.

Jenny O'Neill RN RMHN, Grad Dip Mental Health is a Gestalt Therapist in private practice, Co-Director of the Illawarra Gestalt Centre and a College Member of Gestalt Australia and New Zealand (GANZ). She is also a registered general and psychiatric nurse, a member of the Australian and New Zealand College of Mental Health Nurses and has extensive experience working in the drug and alcohol field in dual diagnosis situations. A proponent of using art as an expressive and creative medium in work with clients, particularly in working with couples, she is a trainer both nationally and internationally. She was Program Co-Chair for the 7th Conference of the Association for Advancement of Gestalt Therapy AAGT in Florida, 2004.

Margherita Spanuolo Lobb, is a psychologist, psychotherapist, and Director of Istituto di Gestalt in Italy (Venice, Rome, Palermo, Ragusa, Siracusa), offering post-graduate Gestalt therapy programs approved by the Minister for the Universities. She is a Gestalt therapy international trainer, particularly interested in co-creative processes in human relations and psychotherapy. Her recent and current scientific aim is to bridge contemporary psychoanalysis and other approaches with Gestalt therapy. She chaired the European Association for Gestalt Therapy (1996-2002), and the Italian Federation of the Associations of Psychotherapy (2003-05). She authored "*Psicologia della Personalità. Genesi delle Differenze Individualli*" (1982), and edited "*Gestalt Therapy. Hermeneutics and Clinical*" and "Gestalt-thérapie Avec des Patients Sévèrement Perturbés" (2005), co-edited with N.Amendt-Lyon "*Creative License. The Art of Gestalt Therapy*" (2003), and has authored many chapters and articles in various languages.

Frank-M. Staemmler, Dipl. Psych., lives in Würzburg, Germany. He has been working as a Gestalt therapist in private practice since 1976, and as a supervisor and trainer since 1981. He has written about sixty articles and book chapters and three books, and has edited five other books. He is a frequent presenter at international conferences and has served as editor of the *International Gestalt Journal* from 2002 to 2006 and as guest editor of the *British Gestalt Journal* (15/2, 2006). He is now coeditor of the new *Studies in Gestalt Therapy: Dialogical Bridges*.

Part I

········

The Secret Language of Intimacy Workshop

Robert G. Lee

Editor's Note:

The web of snarled, painful, debilitating dynamics, in which couples can become entwined, is often mysterious and difficult to understand. Chapters 1 through 5 present a workshop that has been successful in unraveling this web for couples, others who are single and who wish to be in a couple relationship, as well as clinicians who work with couples. It is based in a Gestalt field theory model of shame and belonging that opens avenues to transform couples' experiences of difficulty into opportunities for greater intimacy and connection.

1

The Secret Language
of Intimacy Workshop

━━━

Introduction

Janet was excited when her business trip unexpectedly finished early. It was not yet noon on a Saturday morning in July, and she had managed to wrap up her 5-day consultation trip two days early. She could drive the three hours back home and surprise her husband, Henry, in plenty of time for them to get ready and celebrate with a good time at their favorite restaurant, a causal place with great food and a wonderful atmosphere in which they had enjoyed many tender moments.

Henry had been disappointed that she had had to make this business trip, particularly since she would be away over the weekend. So he would be happy to see her, she mused, and he would be as excited as she to do something fun on this warm summer night.

However, when she arrived home, Henry's greeting was not warm and engaging, as she had expected. Instead he was distant, dismissive, even a bit harsh. When she proposed that they take in their favorite restaurant later that evening, he replied that he couldn't because he didn't have anything to wear. He became angry, saying that she had shrunk the pants that he liked to wear on such occasions. When she pursued, saying that he had other pants and any pair of pants would be fine, he became enraged, yelling that this wasn't the first pair of pants of his that she had ruined and that she never listened or took responsibility for what she did. Janet was crushed. This wasn't the first time that Henry had exploded in anger. His anger terrified her. As in previous such episodes, she didn't know what to do. She pulled herself together and let him know, again, that he needed to do something about his anger, and she left the room. They didn't talk for three days. Janet was very discouraged. It was at times like this that she wasn't sure that her marriage would survive.

And Henry? Let's replay this incident from his perspective. Not that his perspective is any more or less valid than Janet's. Henry had been very disappointed that Janet had responded to her client's rather sudden request for a consultation. He "knew" there were other qualified people in her organization who could have handled the trip. Henry felt that in general Janet let her organization take advantage of her. And this was just another example of that.

It was a summer weekend, and she had been away so much in the spring. The first couple of days that she was away this time he was a bit lost and not very productive. His heart just wasn't into what he was doing. But Saturday morning, he had finally been able to pull himself together and focus on writing a grant proposal, which was always difficult for him to do. He had gotten beyond missing her and was making good progress when in she walked.

What was he supposed to do? He had already switched himself completely around and now he would have to do that again? This just felt like the way things often went—on her time schedule. Couldn't she understand that he needed a consistent schedule to be productive? She just didn't take responsibility for what she did.

He hadn't really trusted her for about a year now, since the time at a dance when she had walked off the dance floor. She frequently would just up and leave when they would have even a minor disagreement, which was extremely frustrating. But that time on the dance floor was in public, and it left him feeling humiliated. Since then he had felt himself at times become distant from her. He wasn't sure that they were going to make it.

What is happening here? How do we understand the knot in which Janet and Henry frequently find themselves? They are clearly very important to each other. And we can empathize with both of their perspectives. Is this just about differences in their perceptual attunement and personal styles? Certainly integrating individual perceptual frameworks and styles is part of the ongoing tasks necessary for success for every couple. And anyone who has been in a couple relationship knows that this is not always an easy endeavor. On the other hand there are couples who seem to manage these tasks, handling the most difficult of differences, involving religion, culture, or other potentially troubling issues as well as differences of personal makeup—again, not that this is easy. There must be more happening here than meets the eye at first glance.

In fact, much of what goes wrong in intimate relationships, from hurt feelings to entrenched defensiveness and stone-walling, has a secret companion with its own language: shame. This language is a secret language. Most people have a sense that it exists, but little sense that they or their partner might be fluent in their own dialect of this language. It is not only a secret language; it is also a language of secrets, not the kind of secrets that accompany conscious, deliberate attempts to mislead another so as to obtain some personal gain at the other's expense. These secrets are much more subtle and most often form without awareness. They are about our yearnings, emanating from the very energy that draws us together. They are often secrets from our self as well. To become aware of these secrets is to risk experiencing shame.

Gestalt field theory gives us a lens that allows us to see this hidden element in relational dynamics and to understand in general the secret language of intimacy, with its component parts of shame and belonging. I have found that understanding this language, particularly the dialect that is spoken in couple member's own relationship, offers an opportunity to transform the often heart-wrenching effects of this hidden companion—which if left unattended lead to disconnection and ultimate separation—into openings for greater connection and greater intimacy.

In the following chapters, Part I of this book, I share with you a workshop of mine that introduces these concepts and facilitates people becoming aware of how these concepts apply to their own lives, in a safe, supportive, even enjoyable/fun atmosphere. The last chapter in this part of the book focuses on demonstrations that I have conducted with volunteer couples, at the end of workshops. As they do in the workshops, the demos present an opportunity to see how this material plays out in actual couple relationships.

2

The Secret Language
of Intimacy Workshop

~~~~

Shame & Belonging

The Secret Language of Intimacy Workshop, which I am about to share with you, has been very successful in opening new possibilities for couples, people interested in a couple relationship, as well as those who work with or would like to work with couples. I started my career in the helping professions as a couples therapist some 30 plus years ago, and this workshop is an integration of my experience, my research on couples and shame (Lee, 1994b), and my writings (e.g., Lee, 1994a, 1996, 2004b). It is influenced by the workshop designs that Gordon Wheeler and I created in working with shame and belonging[1]. Moreover, the material in this workshop is not just theory to me

---

[1] See Lee & Wheeler, 1996, as the initial result of our work together, and see Wheeler, 2002, for another example of a workshop design that emanated from this work.

8 ...

or what helps me organize what I do in my work with clients. This material has been of utmost importance to me in the ongoing success of my own couple relationship. Over the last nine years, I have presented this workshop in a number of locations throughout the world (London, Melbourne, Sydney, Brisbane, Cleveland, Big Sur, Cleveland and other Australian and US locations) and in a variety of time formats from a couple of hours to several days. The form that I share with you here is what I have commonly used in a two day time frame.

A significant design question in constructing workshops for couples is how to help them explore the problems or difficulties in their relationship without becoming triggered and hopelessly lost in a maze of shame. This workshop does just that. It facilitates couples looking at their system and learning about what they do in a manner that is safe and non-threatening. They come away with a different sense of their relationship, with strategies and tools that fit with their new sense. It also allows people to attend who are single and not presently in a relationship or for one partner to attend without the other.

The Initial Exercise Sets the Tone

I open this workshop with an exercise that gives participants a felt sense of the hidden dynamics that can plague couples, mysteriously turning potentially heartfelt, loving, connective interactions into nightmares of frustration, pain and disconnection.

I ask people to pair off—with someone with whom they are not in an intimate relationship. Thus, for the people that come to the workshop as a couple to learn together about and to enrich their relationship, which of course many do, I still ask them to find someone other than their own partner for this exercise. This structure adds to participants' experience of safety since the people in the resulting dyads will not have built up a history of difficult/unresolved interactions with each other. Such a history can lead to an underlying sense of unfairness, resentment and the like, which could be triggered in doing this exercise. Again, the purpose of this exercise is to give people a personal sense, from the inside out, of relationally difficult couple interactions while at the same time maintaining a safe, even fun, environment.

After participants pair off into dyads, I tell them to imagine that they are in a primary relationship with their dyadic partner. Optimally I would like them to imagine that this relationship is a primary love relationship—with a partner that matches their sexual preference. For those participants who have paired off with someone who is of opposite gender than their sexual preference, I extend the option of imagining this relationship to be a very close friendship.[2] Whatever it is, they are to imagine that this relationship is very important to them.

However, I tell them, there is something that is not right with this relationship. I don't know what it is. Perhaps they don't have sufficient time with their partner, or the quality of the time together is lacking in some manner, or something is wrong with the sex in the relationship (if it is a sexual

---

[2] This is frequently necessary because of the gender imbalance in most workshops.

relationship), or something regarding the care of the kids (if they imagine that they have kids) is not being appreciated by their partner. I ask them to take a few minutes by themselves to write about the problem that exists for them in this relationship. By choosing the problem, they are more likely to find something that they care about. This is important for the exercise to work as *it is only when we care that we are susceptible to experiencing shame.* At the same time, because this is an artificial situation, the design offers a buffer against people reaching the depth of caring and possible concomitant shame that can exist when we have developed a full interdependent relationship.

After they have had a few moments to become grounded in what they imagine is problematic with this relationship, I tell them they must turn to their partner and get this problem resolved. It is very important that they find resolution with their partner. Their satisfaction in this relationship is dependent on their finding resolution. However, there is one constraint. They can't talk about the problem, itself, with their partner. They can talk, discuss, interact in any manner they wish with their dyadic partner; they just can *not* mention or refer to their problem in any way. But again, they must get this problem resolved.

As I share with participants a bit later in the workshop, a basic nature of shame is to hide. The experience of shame is the experience that our yearning is unacceptable—silly, shameful, too much, too little, inappropriate, unthinkable. And therefore we believe that it will be met with disgust, disdain, contempt, anger, or perhaps even worse merely disinterest. In short we will not be received. Thus we hide our yearning. As a

Yearning.

result, we can't talk about our yearning directly. This is why couples can have escalating, explosive arguments that seem to come out of nowhere, around such mundane things as on which side of the table the salt shaker should be placed. They have underlying yearnings which they do not feel safe to expose. To further complicate things, they may or may not be aware that they possess a deeper longing. If we have the sense that our yearning will not be received in our larger field, it is extremely difficult, at times impossible, to even be aware of our yearning.

My intent in designing and using this experiment is to duplicate the field conditions that exist when couples are having difficulties communicating. Invariably the workshop participants are thrown into a mini shame attack, into a (hopefully partial) sense that what they care about can not be received. The effect is usually almost immediate. As I walk around the room, I can see people's amusement, on one hand, and their investment and frustration, on the other, in not being able to get their dyadic partner to hear what they feel needs to be heard.

After a bit of time I ask people to wind-up the exercise and return to the larger group. After I apologize for putting them in this position, I ask them to share their experience of doing this exercise, not the content of what happened but what they experienced. Together we create a list. As participants call out what they experienced, I repeat what they say as I write down their reports of their experience on a piece of newsprint. I make sure during this process that I don't miss any offering from anyone in the group. I also never change or interpret what people say. I want to hear their voice, not as it "should be," but as it is. This, of course, also models the process of fully receiving another which is an integral part of the secret language of intimacy.

Each workshop group has its own style of pace and energy with which people report out their experience in the exercise. Sometimes it comes out quickly, and I have to slow people down sufficiently so I can get everyone's voice. Sometimes it starts out slow and then speeds up. This is all important information, indicating the degree to which people were stirred by the exercise, how much it tapped into a deeper shame (sense of not being received) they carry, how safe they feel (individually and as a group), how they hold their shame, and what kind of support I will need to attend to as the workshop proceeds. I continue with the list until there are no more offerings from the group. The following is a sample composite, drawn from the lists that various groups have generated:

List 1: Participant's Experience During Initial Exercise

frustrated, fraudulent, blaming, sad, delicious, avoiding the issue, collusion, close, fantastic, self-blaming, deflated, gagged, impotent, misunderstood, evasive, angry, surprised, well-defended, familiar, wrong, unheard, meeting a dead end, intense, bored, withdrawn, self-righteous, guarded, judging, controlling, superficial, beaten, guilty, superior, exhausting, ignored, lonely, confused, giving in, invisible, distant, generous, vulnerable, hopeful, all roads lead to the same point

As seen, people commonly have a variety of experiences during this exercise, partially depending on the degree to which they were triggered into a mini shame experience. However, there is a dominant trend in these responses—experiences related to not being received.

Shame's Relational Function

To lay the ground for gleaning additional meaning from this list, I ask participants to give me their associations to the word "shame." Again, as participants voice out their associations, I repeat their offerings and write them on a separate sheet of newsprint. The following is a sample of participant's associations:

List 2: Participant's Associations to Shame

> defended, unaware, not good enough, wrong, hot, recoil, defective, wanting to disappear, churning, pain, shunned, shut-down, embarrassed, naked, angry, child-like, scarred, loss of control, vigilant, bad, defiant, judgmental, debilitating, different, raw, withdrawn, trapped, insignificant, hiding, stuck, ostracized, losses, controlling/controlled, vengeful, grief, fight back, impotent, unworthiness, familiar, dirty, paralyzed, victimized, highly sensitive, tantrum, frozen, silenced, humiliated, palpitations, judged, alone, prostrate, avoidant, physical discomfort, rescuer, panic, exposed, puffed-up, self-righteous, black, hatred, insecurity, unlovable, having secrets, shameless, unjust

This list usually comes easily and is much longer than the first. The experience of shame is all too familiar to most of us. The similarity between this list, generated from participants' associations to the word "shame," and the list generated from their experience during the first exercise is always substantial. Comparing the two lists usually brings home to workshop participants the conclusion that their experience in the first exercise had something to do with the phenomenon of shame. Further, it exemplifies the field nature of the experience of shame. That is, shame is not just an individual phenomenon; it has to do with the perceived experience that we are not received, which is influenced in some important way by what is happening around us. For example, people in the workshop had the shame related experiences cited in the first list as a result of the situation in which I placed them, not because of some individual trait.

This is, in fact, the purpose of shame. It is the reason, from an evolutionary perspective, why we are able to experience this affect—why it is part of our survival kit of emotions. Darwin (1872) told us of how emotions provide a social function, important to the survival of our species, as they are an instantaneous analysis of the condition of our field. The seat of their expression is the face, combined with characteristic postures and gestures, which enables large amounts of information to be transmitted between species members over relatively large distances. (see also discussion in Wheeler, 2004) Tomkins (1963), building on Darwin's work, later identified shame as having a special role in intra-psychic dynamics. He proposed that shame regulates our positive affects. For him, the positive affects were interest-excitement and enjoyment-joy, combinations of which encapsulate all of our hopes, dreams, and yearnings—in short, our reasons for living. "The experience of shame is inevitable for any human being insofar as desire outruns fulfillment sufficiently to attenuate interest without destroying it." (p. 185) In a similar vein, Kaufman (1980) reminds us that the only time we are in danger of experiencing shame is when we care. From this, using a Gestalt lens, we can see that the experience of shame is tied to the perception that our yearning is not or will not be received. Shame pulls us back when we don't believe that we will be received and we have insufficient support (internal or from the environment). Thus shame regulates our social field. (Lee, 1994a, 1995, 2001, 2002, 2004; Lee & Wheeler, 1996)

This fits with the more common cultural sense of shame in that when we say to someone "shame on you," we mean that we believe that their actions might hurt another and thus we want them to control, pull back, from their underlying yearnings. However, more importantly, this Gestalt lens brings a new understanding of shame. *The experience of shame is always an attempt to protect, within a relational context.* This is very important as shame is often thought of as a bad or taboo entity and frequently given labels such as "toxic," which externalizes our experience and potentially robs us of our identity.

In order to address the destructive, sometimes crippling side of shame, we must understand how even in such cases the experience of shame is an attempt to protect. In addition, shame holds a precious code of our self-perceived needs and longings and their potential fit with others. *While shame is experienced as information about the self, it is actually information about our perception of the condition of our larger field—of others' ability and interest in receiving us.* This expanded sense of the nature and function of shame can be a powerful force in healing people and is one of the main reasons why this workshop has been so successful.

Further, this new understanding of shame's role in regulating intersubjective interactions offers us new light on the ubiquitous nature of shame in human experience, which is reflected in its many variants, including: shyness, embarrassment, chagrin, humiliation, low self-esteem, feeling ridiculous, sheepishness, discomfort, disconcertedness, abasement, disgrace, ignominy, dishonor, mortification, degradation, self-consciousness, discouragement, and guilt. (Kaufman, 1989; Lewis, 1971; Retzinger, 1987). It means that in any of these circumstances shame is acting to help us pull back because of our perception that the field will not receive our underlying yearning. It is the active ingredient or catalyst in most unawares retroflection, turning our energy back against ourselves, e.g., holding oneself rather than getting held by another (see Lee, 1995).

Belonging

The opposite pole of the experience of not being received, of shame, is the experience of belonging. It is the experience of reception and connection, the experience that this is "my/our world." To help workshop participants have a fresh experience of this pole of human experience, I ask them to return to their dyads and to explore their basic relational yearnings, what they long for from an intimate relationship. To help facilitate an experience of belonging, I give specific instructions of how this dyadic exploration is to occur. Within each dyad there will be a talker and a listener. Talkers will explore their relational yearnings, and listeners are to receive the talkers. More specifically, listeners are to participate in active listening only, feeding back what they hear as it makes sense to the talkers, not to themselves. Listeners are not to add anything, subtract anything, nor make it more or less or to fix anything. They are just there to get what the talkers are trying to say in terms of the talkers' own meaning. Participants decide who will go first as talker and listener, and after they have engaged with each other for sufficient time in this alignment (about 7 minutes), I have them switch roles. List 3 is a composite from various workshops that we have generated together, in a similar fashion as before, of the participants' reports of their exploration of their relational yearnings:

This list usually comes easily also. People usually have some sense of what they want from a relationship. These yearnings are most likely what brought them to this workshop. Interestingly, as a sign of the felt importance of these yearnings, single words are often no longer sufficient as descriptions. People's yearnings are specific, and it is important to get them right, which means using phrases or sentences.

List 3: What Participants Want From a Relationship?
What Are Their Yearnings?

accepted and loved, to be interested in me, tenderness, open, find me exciting and interesting, experienced sparingly, scooped up, trust, nonjudgmental support, love me warts and all, seen and held, passion, freedom to be in the present moment, this is who I am, attended to, prized, you will hang around and keep looking, delicious novelty, loving gaze, to share, seen and not abandoned, to be cherished, spontaneity, discovery, understand my struggle, closeness and space, to merge, security, see me—not an illusion of me, to be acknowledged, to be desired, to laugh, being able to say the unspeakable, peace, empathy, wanting to give attention, acts of generosity, forgiveness, feeling of deep connection, commitment, reliability, to be honored and respected, being with—in whatever way, shape or form, environment where I can continue to blossom

As mentioned, having people explore and share their relational yearnings in their dyads serves a further purpose in addition to potentially putting them in touch with why they came to this workshop. My hope is that participants acquired, in the course of doing this experiment, a small sampling of what they yearn for in relationships—at least to the extent that they felt well received and felt that their receiving of their dyadic partner was valued. This is an essential piece of the experience of connection and belonging. If that kind of experience was indeed generated in doing this last experiment, even in a small way, we have a whole new body of information that we can explore, including how people reacted to this experience. Thus I ask them to report out what it felt like in their dyad to have someone listen to them as they explored their relational yearnings. And the list below summarizes their responses:

List 4: How Participants Felt in Being Listened to in Their Dyad

> liked being asked questions, moving away, resonating, vague, sadness—saying things I do not have, wanting agreement, engaged, selfish, frightened by my vulnerability, less comfortable, disbelief, unclear, feels like I want too much, like being heard, freeing, happy, not going to be enough, exposed/pleased, anxiety, lightness, expecting from me, self conscious, comfortable, uncertain, vulnerability/positive experience deepening, embarrassed, energized, edgy—wanting to say & wanting to hold back, tearful, stupid in thinking this is even possible, exposed/awkward, tantalizing, move from a sense that I deserve all these to a sense of cautiousness and restraint, clarifying, safe, open, affirming, validating, supportive, feeling understood

In fact, the exploration and sharing of the relational yearnings exercise with a dyadic partner does, in the least, raise the potential of connection for participants. Two themes predominate in participants' reports of what occurred for them, one being the experience of "really being listened to," including how that facilitates a deeper exploration of one's experience. The other dominant theme is a cautiousness and/or disbelief that this kind of receptivity is possible at all. Examples of the latter include "stupid in thinking this is even possible," "feels like I want too much," "embarrassed," and "wasting my breath." In many of these cases you can hear expressions of shame (stupid, too much, embarrassed, wasting) at work, attempting to pull people back from their yearnings when they don't feel there is sufficient possibility of their yearnings being received. Of course, this reflects the difficultly that many of us have had in securing this kind of connection in our lives in general. It also is further information about the kind of support people in the workshop need, just to contemplate this kind of yearned-for experience. To add meaning to this list I ask participants to voice out their associations to the words "connection" and "belonging" (see List 5 on the next page).

Again, in this list, the same two kinds of experiences are found—the experience of finding reception and the experience of doubting that such reception is possible. However, in generating this latter list, participants are usually more able to imagine and express this most desirable pole of human existence, perhaps because the list is constructed around an imagined state and not one that people have to contemplate or deal with in the present. The bulk of the list not only includes descriptions of people's imagined experience of belonging and connection but also how important they hold these experiences to be for their quality of life, e.g., "absolutely necessary," "one's birth right," and "necessary for survival."

List 5: *Participant's Associations to Connection and Belonging*

unknown, support, acceptance, groundedness, easy, peace, identity, embraced, not really accepted, seen, relaxing, unexperienced, visibility, necessary for survival, voice, closeness, being confident, sharing, unlimited possibilities, truth, comfort, common beliefs, excited, not quite trusting of, trust, choicefulness, potential, expanding process, love, anxious, gratefulness, freedom, unsophisticated, spirit, warmth, real democracy, gratitude, being understood, joy, connection, unfamiliar, presence, comfortable in self, welcome, not believable, strength, my deepest yearning, relief, unmasked, friendship, amazed, ability to grow, OK, vulnerable, confrontation, knowing, absolutely necessary, ease, openness, wussy words, shameful, the way it should be, life, feminine, credible others, boundaries, physical comfort, safety, nurturing, community, honesty, not in my experience, babble, affection, cannot relate, believing, conflict resolution, secure, intimacy, compassion, respect, one's birth right, healing, complete, grief and loss, release of creativity, unity, just words, togetherness, empty talk, interdependence, full

While smaller in number, the experience of doubting whether connection and belonging are possible is represented also, with phrases such as "just words," "wussy words," and "empty talk." Again, these are indications of the difficulty people have had in finding this kind of experience. And again words like "wussy," "just," and "empty" reflect the possibility of shame at work to pull people back from their yearnings in this direction. Like with all shame, the strength of the expression of shame is an <u>indication of the intensity of the underlying yearning that is being reined in.</u>

Shame and Belonging
The Poles of Human Experience

Now we have the experiences of shame and belonging, the poles of human existence, present in the workshop. And importantly, we have them in a manner in which they can be touched. It is now possible to offer the possibility that all human, let alone couple, experience is some combination of these two experiences —the possibility that this is what the secret language of intimacy is all about. [*Is it possible that an underlying component of every interaction*, particularly in a couple system, where our needs and wants are most keen, *is a measuring of and responding to*, with or without awareness, *our sense of the extent to which connection and belonging are occurring and/or are possible and at the same time of the degree to which we are experiencing or anticipate disconnection and shame?*] And thus is it possible that in every couple interaction we find ourselves engaged, again with or without awareness and depending on the joint resources and condition of our self and our partner, in some combination of the language and behavior of belonging and/or the language and behavior of shame?

My own research on couples (Lee, 1994b) bears out that, in fact, these are the poles of couple experience. Couples who had developed a high degree of *emotional safety*—such that they felt safe enough most of the time to bring up their deepest concerns, feelings, desires, or problems, had clear expectations of each other, and in general thought of each other as best friends— were also found to have high marital satisfaction, be affectionate with each other, have a fulfilling sexual connection, exhibit low negativity in their interactions, and report that they have good problem-solving capacity. This group of couples, which exhibited so many indications of connection and belonging, were found to have *low ground shame*[3]. The opposite was true for couples with *high ground shame*. They scored at the opposite end of the scale on all of the above mentioned variables— indicative of a low sense of connection and belonging.

Gottman (1994), from his extensive research on couples, reports similar findings. A major criterion he finds for couples' developing satisfying relationships, and not eventually breaking up, is that both members experience four out of five interactions between them as positive. His findings suggest that in successful couples, which he labels as "masters," each couple member's experience is important to the other, and they take care of one another. Gottman reports that in all couples, partners do a high degree of bidding for each other's attention in small ways in everyday interaction. In "masters" couples, the bidding is met

---

[3] The term "ground shame" refers to shame that has been linked with various affects, needs, or ways of being in the world such that when one experiences these, shame is automatically experienced. This is explained further in succeeding paragraphs. "Ground shame" is what Kaufman (1989) refers to as "internalized shame." I prefer to use "ground" to better reflect the relational aspect of this phenomenon, as "ground" refers to our perceived sense of our connectedness in our larger field.

with the partner turning toward the bidder with interest 96% of the time as opposed to only 36% of the time in couples that do not have successful relationships. Moreover, "masters" couple partners support each other when they are in conflict. And equally importantly, they attend to repairing the damage after conflicts.

Ground Shame

But how is it that some couples are able to exist mostly in the experience of belonging while others find themselves entrenched at the other end of this polarity of couple experience? The answer lies in the couple partners' past experience and the resulting sense that they have developed of the possibility that belonging can or cannot truly exist. When we have had repeated or severe enough instances occur in which we are not received, this sense of the world becomes part of our ground. However, the ground structures that form, that then guide us in understanding and behaving in future interactions, employ an indirect path toward this end—a path involving shame.

Remember that it is shame's job to pull us back from acting on our yearnings when we perceive that we might not be received and we do not have sufficient support (internal or external). With instances of repeated or severe enough lack of reception (including extreme and lesser forms of abuse, neglect, loss, or sustained hardship), shame links with our yearning (affect, need, way of being in the world) that is not received such that any time that yearning starts to appear, shame will intervene to pull us away from our yearning. Thus shame, in such cases, becomes part of our ground.

Nathanson (1987) discusses the ubiquitous nature of shaming stimuli that surround all of us. He suggests that the warlike battles in which marital partners attempt to settle their differences by gaining dominance over each other have their roots in shaming experiences encountered during their earlier years, as far back as their adolescence and childhood. Nathanson argues that such experiences teach people the potential of shame as a weapon in interpersonal conflicts, long before they are even old enough to enter into a couple relationship.

But the learning process here is not just about acquiring the skill of using shame as an interpersonal weapon. Notice that what is really being taught in such early experiences is that openness, inclusion, trust, and dialogue—connection and belonging—are not possible in given instances. The result is our unaware attempt to protect ourselves (and others in our relational field) through the development of ground shame.

As an example of developing ground shame, consider an infant, Johnny, whose parents have experienced a great deal of trauma in their lives. When Johnny becomes distressed and cries, that reactivates his parents' sense of trauma and they either pull away from him or shame him directly (e.g., "big boys don't cry," even though he is only an infant). In these moments, in response to the unreceptive condition of his larger field, Johnny will use shame to pull himself away from the part of him that is not being received. This is what happens naturally when the environment does not respond to us, and we do not have sufficient internal support. However, with enough such instances, shame will attach to the experience of distress (forming what Perls calls an "introject"—see Lee, 1995), and Johnny will then automatically experience shame whenever he experiences distress. In time he will lose awareness that he is experiencing distress and only experience shame. In the process, he loses a voice for his distress.

The more that the significant people in our environment do not respond to our needs, do not meet us or understand us (possibly because of their own experiences of trauma and past lack of reception), the more ground shame we develop. Again, each piece of acquired ground shame is in effect a belief that our underlying yearning can not be responded to, and is put in place as an attempt to protect our self or other(s) in our field. Thus ground shame is our creative adjustment (a concept that I will develop further later) to our perception of the ongoing lack of interest or ability of our environment to respond to us in particular situations, in which we disown our yearning through attaching shame to it, making it part of "not my world."

3

The Secret Language
of Intimacy Workshop

◢◢◢◢

Shame Attacks

To this point in the workshop we have laid the ground for exploring the poles of couple experience—shame and belonging. And we have explored how shame can work as a momentary control and how it can link with a consistently or severely unreceived part of us to form ground shame, in our attempt to protect our self and/or others in our field.

Shame Attacks and the Behavior That Follows

Unfortunately, when we develop ground shame, we then acquire a much higher ongoing risk of experiencing a "shame attack." Shame does not extinguish our yearning; it just pulls us away from it when it materializes. In the example of the previous chapter, after Johnny develops ground shame he will still have instances in which he is distressed. He just will not be able to experience his distress. Instead when distress comes he will be flooded with shame (a shame attack). Because shame is so corrosive, he will develop strategies to attempt to escape the experience of shame, trying to hide it from others as well as himself. Perhaps he will learn to become angry or enraged at such times or to become critical, be contemptuous or blame. Or he might withdraw and stonewall others. Or he could learn to control, be over polite, use sarcastic humor, or flee to some form of addiction or obsession—whatever it takes in his attempt to deal with the experience of shame. Of course, whatever strategies he develops have to work within his environment. In one environment stonewalling might work, where as becoming enraged won't, or vice versa, depending on the interactive effect and value of each in the given environment. (Again, I will develop this further later.)

Most of us develop some amount of ground shame. Not many of us are fortunate enough to be born to parents who themselves have low ground shame. Further, every culture has developed cultural ground shame, because of the culture's past trauma, and developed strategies to cope with such ground shame that then get woven into the requirements of membership. This includes our gender culture. Thus ground shame, shame attacks, and strategies to deal with shame attacks are part of the set of experiences and skills that couple members bring to their relationship when they couple.

To help couple members to be successful in finding a path to spending more of their time in connection and belonging, we must help them face, understand and heal their ground shame. This is not an easy task as by definition their ground shame is *example*.

shameful. To ask people to even get near their ground shame is to put them at risk of experiencing a shame attack. But in fact, the perspective of shame that we have developed in this workshop offers a new way to hold our ground shame—not as something shameful, but as our attempts to protect our self and others. We do not carry ground shame because we are bad people, but because our environment (due to its own past trauma or differences in makeup and/or experience) has not been able to respond to us. Thus we have the opportunity in this workshop to start the process of undoing our ground shame, the process of exploring whether our underlying yearnings can now be responded to. But to do this we must first face the shame that we carry that often keeps us from even knowing that our yearnings exist.

To support participants in this process, I normalize having ground shame by sharing an example from my own life. The example that I often use occurred about a year and a half into my relationship with my wife, while we were courting. We met dancing, and dancing has always been an important part of our being together. For many years we would dance several times a week. One evening when we were to go dancing, I had to work late, and we decided to meet at the dance, with my wife arriving earlier and me joining her after I finished work. Well, that particular day turned out to be a long one, and I was a bit depleted and in need of a little TLC (tender loving care) by the time that I showed up at the dance. However, I wasn't quite aware of this. Most likely this wouldn't have been an issue if my wife and I had gone to the dance together, because we like to start off dancing with each other for a number of dances before we start dancing with other people. However, when I arrived at the dance, the dance floor was crowded, and I couldn't locate my wife. I tried dancing with a few other people, knowing I would eventually hook up with my wife. But that evening it didn't feel good to be dancing with someone other than my wife. Again, I needed a little TLC, even though I wasn't aware of that. Now my wife is a very good dancer and people love to dance with her. So when I finally sighted my wife (she hadn't seen me as yet), she would quickly be swept up by another dancer as soon as the music of one song stopped and before the next song began. I tried going over close to where she was dancing and waiting for the next song to come along. But on my way there I was asked to dance myself and couldn't say no. When the dance ended and I looked around; my wife had disappeared again. At this point I gave up and sat down and watched the dancing. While sitting I spotted her dancing. She was having fun as she usually does dancing. But now my need, of which I wasn't really aware, became shamed. Instead of enjoying watching her dance as I usually do. I found myself noticing how she wasn't dancing "correctly." She wasn't "anchoring" as she should; her arm was too tight... The more I looked; the more I noticed.

Soon the overhead lights came on. This club always had an intermission during the evening in which there would be some sort of dance demonstration given by a local professional. My wife spotted me, and came over and sat with me. Almost immediately, I found myself "sharing" with her all the "mistakes" that I had been noticing of her dancing. Of course, I was only "trying to be helpful." (So I thought.) My wife looked at me with an innocence and curiosity. And with a matching tone, she said to me, "Are you criticizing me?" The message in her look and tone was something like "I don't understand; how does this fit in our relationship?" This support threw me back on my process, which I most likely couldn't have managed without that sense of connection. I realized that I was in a shame attack, and that I needed something from her, and further I needed to ask her for it. I remember feeling a sudden sense of terror in that asking her would expose my vulnerability and she might not have what I wanted or want to give it to me. But because of the sense of connection I received with her look and tone I summoned up all the courage I could muster and I asked her, "Do you love me?" A warm smile came over her face; she leaned over and hugged me and said fully, "Is that what this is about? Of course, I love you." With this, I got the TLC that I needed, and we had a great time the rest of the evening.

With this example of my own ground shame as support for participants, I remind them that most of us have times when we are off-balance without sufficient support, for which we have developed favorite strategies, like my using criticism when I could not get the TLC that I needed. I then ask them to return to their dyads to explore, in the same structure of talker and listener as earlier, what their experience is and what strategies they have developed to use when they are off-balance without sufficient support—perhaps what they found themselves doing in the initial exercise. The following is a sampling of the lists that have been generated after this exercise, when people report out in the larger group what they became aware of during their exploration:

List 6: Participants' Off-Balanced Strategies & Behaviors

intellectualize, give up on my own need, crying, eat, push other away, appearing to remain engaged, attacking, blame, act self-reliant, internal eye rolling, deflecting, drink, being anxious, false light heartedness, sarcastic, obsess, pick on the other, maximize how bad the other is, sulking, rage, create new game, projecting my need on to the other, shut down, arrogant, become big brother, become self-righteous, criticizing, overwork, beat myself up, being very reasonable, catastrophize, go to bed, fear of being alone, watch TV or play video games, stonewall, rescuing, feeling useless, get crabby and leave (jet), over-exercise, be less than I am, act helpless or needy, exaggerated sense of responsibility, do not breathe, acquiescing, take on role of victim, make demand of God, buy something, worry about health, pressure self with unreasonable expectations, demean others, perfection-ism, controlling, dissociating, freeze, become over polite/supportive, pretend things are OK, smile, revengeful, avoid, escape, eat chocolate, vindictive, rebellious, do what the other isn't, hiding, tough, self pity, judge others, joke

This list is always very rich, creative and diverse. The openness with which people participate in this exercise shows the degree of support that we have been able to develop in the workshop to this point. In looking at the list, we quickly get a fuller, more appreciative sense of the usually very private experience that most of us deal with alone—the experience of being off-balance without sufficient support. It is this kind of experience which holds our highest risk of being in a shame attack.

It is easy at this point to bring home the point that we do not have this experience and we do not engage in these behaviors because we are "bad," "inadequate," or "mentally disturbed" people. Instead, we find our self in this place and exhibit these behaviors because of our underlying sense, with or without awareness, that we do not have sufficient support.

And here is the kicker. *We are doomed to find ourselves at times engaged in these strategies and behaviors, treating others and ourselves in this manner, unless we can become aware of when we are off-balance without sufficient support and we can figure out ways to get our self sufficient support.* In a couple relationship, this might mean testing out whether our partner can respond to our underlying yearning. Or it might mean finding a way to support our self when our partner is off-balance and experiences a shame attack. Importantly, it means learning about and educating our partner, in general, about our process and our underlying, hidden vulnerability that can occur at such times. And it means becoming aware of our partner's process in a similar manner. But, again, it starts with knowing and owning that we are off-balance, which means facing the shame that can come with that experience.

This is usually the end of the first day of the workshop. And

I send participants home with the homework of exploring what kind of support they, and their partners, need when they are off-balance without sufficient support, in order not to resort to the strategies and behaviors that they have enumerated in the list that we have generated together.

At the beginning of the workshop, the next day, I spend some time learning about and being with what has been evoked in participants from the previous day's experience. We covered an immense amount the previous day, and I do not want participants to be alone with their experience. Being alone with what has been evoked in us can, in itself, lead to a reinforcement of old experience that our environment cannot respond to us. On the positive side, among the reports that I often get are statements that, during the previous evening after the workshop, some participants were able to start a different type of conversation/interaction with their partners that was more connective, endearing, and hopeful.

Origins of Our Favorite Off-Balanced Strategies

Again, shame is a relational phenomenon, not an individual phenomenon. This is particularly true of the ground shame that we carry as well as the strategies and behavior that we have developed to attempt to cope with times that we are off-balance without sufficient support. Our ground shame and coping strategies are an ongoing relational link to the people and situation from which they came. They are our creative adjustment in times of insufficient support from the people around us that we depend on and in turn who depend on us—

and thus to the experience of our self that we carry and the strategies we develop must fit within our field context.

On a simple level, our creative strategies to deal with our ground shame, emanating from times of insufficient reception, may be nonverbal learnings copied from parents. For example, a child whose parent flies into anger when the parent becomes scared, because the parent was never received during his/her own childhood at such times, might also develop ground shame around being scared and come to have a "temper," like his/her parent, to camouflage and attempt to deal with times when he/she becomes afraid or uncertain.

However, a child's creative adjustment might also be more complex. Remember that the reason for acquiring ground shame is that the child is not sufficiently received in some needed manner. That means that the family system hasn't been able to sufficiently and/or consistently notice and respond to the child in a particular area. Most likely this has happened because particular family members or the family system, as a whole, has been off-balance due to their own ground shame that is triggered at such times. Thus, a significant component of a child's creative adjustment, to handle his/her ground shame, is to emotionally, in someway, hold together one or more members in the family system.

For example, a client of mine carried a sense that she was dumb. When she felt dumb she would isolate herself, stonewalling others, a strategy that worked in her family of origin but which had become a problem in her marriage. Her brothers and sisters (seven, in number) all had advanced degrees—PhDs,

MDs, or law degrees. One brother had two PhDs; a sister had a law degree and a PhD; several of her siblings were well published. She had made it through college, but academics never really interested her. Her interests lay in the natural healing arts—massage, herbs—and in other areas that she associated with Polynesian culture. She prided herself as being a "free spirit." Growing up, she reported, her family looked down on her because she had little interest in academics. They thought of her as dumb. My sense of this young woman was that she was very bright. She quickly grasped the intricacies of anything I said to her and she would respond thoughtfully and creatively.

It turned out that her grandmother was born and raised in Polynesia in a situation of poverty, of which her grandmother was very ashamed. Her grandmother was able to escape her plight, as a young woman, through her brightness and education. She rose to the status of full professor at a major university and was in constant demand as an academic consultant within her field. This brought her a great deal of status. Academics and professionalism had become the family strategies and resources for dealing with life's stresses. On the other hand, anything to do with the family's Polynesian roots was considered taboo. Thus in effect my client was carrying an appreciation of her Polynesian roots for the rest of the family. Her adapted coping style of stonewalling worked in the family, as the family could not tolerate being exposed to the taboo associated with her interests. And most probably they could allow her to continue with these interests, as long as they didn't have to know too much about it, because underneath the taboo they too most likely carried a yearning to have a connection with their roots. Thus her ground shame and coping strategy held a function for her family, most probably for her grandmother in particular. The price for her to hold the family together in this way was for her to feel dumb.

Returning to the workshop, with this story as ground, I ask participants to go back to their dyads to explore whether their favorite off balance strategies had similar roots. Again, in the context of listener and follower, they are to explore who in their family of origin, or in whatever setting in which they adapted their strategy, might have been held together, and in what manner, by their feeling this way about themselves and employing this strategy. List 7 is a sampling of what participants have reported from their exploration in this exercise.

This exercise gives participants another experience of shame's relational nature and helps them embrace their own sense of shame in terms of the function it might have served in their family rather than as a sign of their own individual failing.

List 7: Role and Effect in Family of Origin

1) scapegoat - served as pressure valve for family

2) identified patient - still in therapy - "why is she so slow?" saves others from dealing with their troubles

3) being less than I am - helped dad maintain his sense of being OK

4) wrong to expect things of others - mom was overwhelmed and limited in what she could give

5) must look after others first - became mom's planner, shopper, and cook - the organized girl - equated with love, cleaned plates - mom was severely depressed

6) working hard - "good education would help you deal with whatever the problem was" - both parents worked, family poor, helped them deal with their load - no memories of fun

7) took on mom's struggles, sparing others in her place, became known as the angry child - mom alcoholic, dad absent - camouflaged the real problems

8) freeze - both parents very fragile, needed me not to be a real person

4

The Secret Language
of Intimacy Workshop

Couple Shame Cycles

So far in the workshop we have been exploring the dynamics of shame and belonging within us as single individuals in the context of interacting with others. But of course the real world is more complicated than that. The other people in our environment, our couple partners in particular, are not mere objects who are not affected by us or others. They are people just like us, who can become off-balanced and who carry their own ground shame to one extent or another.

What often happens when one member of a couple becomes off-balance, falls into a shame attack which pulls him/her back from his/her yearning, and then resorts to the strategies and behavior he/she has developed for such occasions, is that such behavior and strategies, like my being critical at the dance with my wife, then activate the other couple member's shame. For example, imagine if my wife would have become shamed rather than just curious following my critical remarks to her at the dance. Once shamed, the second couple member will then most likely resort to his/her own strategies and behaviors that he/she has developed to escape shame. For example, if my wife would have responded by telling me the mistakes that I make when dancing, or defamed my character—"You are always so critical; you just like to dominate people." Or if she became polite and distant, or sullen, or contemptuous, or got up and left. The result is that the first couple member very likely becomes even more shamed. This in effect confirms to the first couple member that in fact his/her underlying yearning will not be received and is shameful. And he/she then, in an attempt to escape his/her increased sense of shame, ups the ante and responds in a more shaming manner. For example, if my wife had responded to my criticism with criticism of my dancing and I had responded to that by saying something like "You just can't handle constructive criticism." Or if I would have said "You are just like your mother; I try to be helpful and you just have to control the conversation." Of course, when the ante is raised the second couple member gets a heavier dose of shame and must respond in kind. And thus the situation escalates into more and more shaming, painful, and isolating exchanges, in which partners more and more attempt to distance themselves from their underlying yearnings for connection.

When this happens it means that both couple members are off-balance without sufficient support, both needing the other to recognize and respond nurturantly to their vulnerability. And since they are both off-balance, neither one can give the other what the other is seeking, even though they might have it to give if they weren't off-balance and could recognize the other's vulnerability. (see Balcolm, Lee, & Tager, 1995)

To help give participants an experiential understanding of this phenomenon, I ask participants to go back into their dyads and explore what happened in the original exercise with their dyadic partner. In response to the strategy that one of them employed, did the other engage in a counter strategy that then was met with a heightening of the strategy employed by the first person and so on? I also suggest that participants can reflect on other relationships, either current or past, for examples of this kind of interaction. In this exercise, I have participants be more interactive as talker and listener. List 8 gives a sampling of what participants have found.

This exercise is usually an eye-opener to participants. They get a chance to see how what they do as a means of protecting themselves can unintentionally off-balance their partner. And they see how what happens between themselves and their partner in a couple shame cycle cuts the support from both of them, which further, often wrongly, reinforces for both of them that what they seek is not possible to obtain. The language of shame, in such couple cycles, revolves around hiding one's desire for connection and doing something to knock the other person off-balance.

Complementarity

List 8: Participant's Couple Shame Cycles

---

1) On not being heard one member of a dyad rolled her eyes. Her partner reported that caused him to abandon his own needs and he then tried to fix the situation by making deals, which left him feeling very off-balance. The effect on the first dyad member was to become further irritated, and the cycle spiraled.

2) A married couple reported that a common interaction between them occurs when she says, "I don't like ... (something that he is doing.)" This stirs in him a sense of inadequacy, and he finds himself defensively doing it more. She then imagines that "he doesn't care." She then gets angry and tells him in a stronger manner how she doesn't like what he is doing. This just increases his sense of inadequacy, and he finds himself doing it even more.

3) One participant became confused and scattered during the exercise. In response his partner became irritated and expressed that by being logical. The first partner reported the apparent togetherness of the second partner caused him to feel dumb and he became more scattered, which further irritated the second partner who became disdainfully logical.

Complementarity

For many years, couples theorists (e.g., Zinker, 1983) and experienced couples therapists have recognized the phenomenon of complementarity, in which couple members select each other, most often without awareness, based on what they need to complete in themselves. Of course, couple members must be enough alike in order to find each other and to couple. However, according to this concept, a significant element in attraction is the possession of complementary differences in life views and strategies (e.g., planning/scheduling activities vs. being spontaneous; verbally oriented vs. nonverbally oriented; taking risks vs. being cautious). These complementary pairings of differences in couples occur because we perceive we need, most frequently without awareness, to find someone who has what we don't have and in turn who doesn't have what we do have. And if we have primarily developed one end of a polarity, what we haven't developed is the other end of the same polarity. However, after selection, as a couple's relationship evolves in the course of living with one another, these differences can become major sources of conflict.

Looking at complementarity through the lens of shame and belonging, and understanding the secret language of intimacy unlocks some of the mysteries of the troubles that couples can encounter around this phenomenon. This also offers a deeper understanding of the complexity of one variant of couple shame cycles.

As is easy to deduce, in essence, couples have three options when they discover their complementarity:

1) They can understand that they have picked well in finding someone that has another way of being in the world that they wanted/needed to learn about, and use each other as teachers.

2) They can divide up tasks such that they each handle only the tasks that require their own evolving competence.

3) They can proselytize, trying to convert each other to their "non taboo" way of being in the world.

The decision as to which option is chosen is usually made without awareness. Most couples employ all three of these strate-gies, in varying degrees, depending on the area in question and /or on the emotional resources of the couple at any given time.

The first option requires low ground shame in the area of the complementary pairing—a sense that each person is OK, the other's person's differences aren't threatening and learning from the other is an adventure. As has been recognized in the field, this option helps both partners to become more well rounded individuals in two ways. Not only do they both learn some of the skills of the other, but in addition what usually occurs is that the whole becomes greater than the sum of the parts. Through their intersubjective development, a new way of being in the world emerges, which has been facilitated by their jointly having access to the combination of their individual views and skills.

Couples often resort to the second option, of a division of labor, to handle at least some of their tasks. For example this frequently occurs along gender lines. And this may work well for them. However, when they rely solely on this strategy as an overall method of handling problems then they limit their growth as individuals, which may become problematic in terms of their overall marital satisfaction as well as their satisfaction with their individual lives.

A reliance on option three represents having the highest amount of ground shame around the concerned areas and perhaps in general. It frequently means that, for one or both couple members, some aspect of their partner's complementary way of being in the world is taboo for them. Thus, when they get close to their partner's complementary way of being in the world they run into their associated taboo. Hence processing these areas of their relationship becomes almost impossible as one or both continually are at an elevated risk of experiencing shame attacks and engaging in the behavior and strategies that they use to camouflage and to cope with shame. When both couple members have a taboo (i.e., each having high ground shame) around the opposite of their own skill (way of being in the world), then when one couple member becomes off-balanced and resorts to his/her coping behavior and strategies, it is highly likely that the other will be triggered. Consequently they frequently find themselves in the middle of a couple shame cycle, usually without any awareness of the underlying, hidden factors that are driving their interaction.

As we learned earlier, in a couple shame cycle, both partners are off-balance. Neither has sufficient support. Neither has a voice to tell the other of their underlying vulnerability or desire for connection, let alone their appreciation of the other. Either both are caught in an adversarial struggle for survival, attempting to discredit/blame/off-balance the other as a way of camouflaging their own experience of shame, or one or both partners have given up and are enduring their misery in isolation. If your underlying vulnerability/need/yearning is shamed, there is little other option.

For example, if a couple is entrenched in slinging hurtful barrages of blame and accusations at one another, we might expect them to understand the (otherwise obvious) fact that emotionally crippling and/or dominating their partner never leaves their partner in a position from which the kind of connection that they desire is easily forthcoming. But when one is off-balance, and in the throes of a shame attack, this simple logic cannot be grasped. And the double-bind quality of a couple shame cycle around complementarity is that to some extent, each couple member is simultaneously both attracted to and repulsed by the other's way of being in the world. The tip off that a couple's conflict might be rooted in their respective ground shame, in this manner, is to employ the common technique of asking them what attracted them to each other and to listen for similarities to what they are having difficulty with.

The marvel, in this case, is what it takes to survive under these circumstances. In this light, eruptions, entrenched behavior, and the like can be seen as a sign of the strength of the bond between couple members in their ongoing struggle to deal with these hidden elements. What is lacking is sufficient support—in several ways. This is support that couple members cannot give each other when they are both off-balance.

First, couple members usually need support for their resistance to their partner's way of being in the world. They, of course, developed their taboos in a relational context, most often in their family of origin because of some individual, family, or cultural trauma, which has led to a conflicting way of being in the world. Attempting to change their belief, undo the taboo, too quickly is often experienced as dangerous, immoral, or (on a deeper level) a betrayal of a significant person, their family, or a culture to which they belong. Thus, this process takes time and support for partners to proceed at the pace that they can handle, again something that couple members can't give each other when they are off-balance.

Support tasks associated with this process include support for couple members to develop a tolerance for their partner's complementary way of being in the world—that it is a valid way of being in the world even if it is not their way; support for partners to begin owning their attraction to this "taboo" way of being in the world; and support for developing a tolerance to the shame that they automatically experience when they encounter their partner's way of being in the world.

Here we can think of the Gestalt notion of *responsibility*, which means having *the ability to respond*. We can not be responsible until we have developed the ability to respond. However, developing the ability to respond is shaped by the condition of the field in which we have learned. Thus, said another way, couples caught in these kinds of entanglements have developed an ability to respond that is built on the belief that they must do without sufficient support in some manner, that such support is not possible. They don't know how to invite it, and they don't know how to give it at such times. Without such support, they do not have the ability to respond and they are not responsible.

To return to the workshop, my purpose here, in the time

frame that we have available, is to expose participants to this concept in such a manner that they can rub against it and even have some fun with it, in the process exploring areas, in a safe atmosphere, that might hold some shame for them. So, to introduce participants to this area and facilitate their acquiring a sense of how complementarity applies in their own life, I have them return to their dyads and, in the same, now familiar, talker/listener format, I have them explore the complements between them and their partner in present or past relationships. The following is a sample of the lists that we have generated together when they return to the larger group:

List 9: Complementarity in Participants' Relationships

> *conformist—non-conformist; leader—follower; taskmaster —atmosphere master; worrier—laid-back; traditional religion/spirituality—alternative religion/spirituality; open— closed; work—play; adult—child; stable—volatile; cleaner/organizer—casual living; social—introvert; fixer— analyzer; worker/planner—having no agenda; thrifty— impulsive buying; spontaneous—consistent; politically oriented—family oriented; dreamer—realist; zoned out— paying attention; rule abider—rebellious*

Creating this list offers an opportunity to touch people's shame in a way that we can have some innocent fun with this material. At this point a great deal of safety has been established in the workshop, which facilitates being lighter, which in turn enables the participants to go further with tolerating their own shame. The key is supporting and normalizing feelings of unease, fear, even revulsion toward the complement of one's developed way of being in the world that people find and must deal with in their partners and, at the same time, modeling a tolerance, even appreciation for this "taboo" polarity. Thus, I want to show a respect for both sides of any complementary pairing as well as for the power of this phenomenon in general.

I start this process of support, as we begin to construct the above list, by mentioning a polarity that exists between my wife and myself and joking about my unease with her style as well as my respect for it. As complementary pairings are reported by participants for the list above, they are of course often stated with labels from the perspective of the value system of the person offering the report. For example, someone might say, "neat— sloppy," in which one side of the polarity is valued (e.g., "neat") and the other side is devalued (e.g., "sloppy"). I will often say, in a light manner, in response to such an offering "Hmm, I wonder which side of this polarity you represent?" And perhaps I will playfully join them in their dislike/revulsion of the opposite polarity by saying "That really is disgusting isn't it?" But then I will say, "But I bet there are others here who think the other side is disgusting." And then I will help participants to find a label for the polarity that is disgusting/shameful to them which would feel good to someone with the other polarity.

This exercise, as well as the last, offers opportunities for participants to integrate the material that has come before in the workshop. Participants often report at this stage that they are starting to "get" what this workshop is all about.

5

The Secret Language
of Intimacy Workshop

~~~~

Support & Demos

Support

The journey that we have taken together in this workshop enables participants to get an experienced-based understanding of the importance of support in couple interactions. *In order for couples to develop successful relationships they need to be as interested in the quality of their partner's experience as they are in their own.* They also need to be able to share with their partner what they need on an ongoing basis as they discover it. Part of mastering the secret language of intimacy is learning to read your and your partner's signs of possible shame and to understand when you or your partner is off-balance without sufficient support.

As a final exercise in the workshop, I have participants return to their dyads and, again in the structure of talker and listener, I have them explore what support they and/or their

partner in their life (if they have a partner) need in the
interactions between them. They do this in two rounds, first
focusing on what their own needs for support are. And then in a
second round exploring what their partner's needs for support
might be. The following is a sample of the two lists that we have
generated together after this exercise:

List 10: My Support Need

*take care of myself, understand my intentions, be able to get
a break then get myself together and come back, be able to
talk about what isn't safe, partner to hang in beyond the
fight part, quiet moments with spouse—on porch swing after
he's shaved, yoga/energy, enough contact with others, listen
to me, establish traditions, friends, my dogs, help me out
with my paper work and with practical things, journal
writing, no active addictions, social/recreational/spiritual
activities, hear me, my therapist, doing some home repairs
and laughing, support group for other, times of just being
nutsy*

Looking at these two lists is revealing. The list of one's
partner's support needs is frequently more relationally and
connectively supportive than the list of one's own supportive
needs, which is often more self-supportive in character. This
tends to be particularly true when participants as a group have
reported more of a sense of doubting that belonging is really
possible, earlier in the workshop. I believe this is indicative of
how difficult it is to even think about asking for a supportive

connection before one has experienced that such is possible. Processing this discrepancy between the lists in the larger group helps participants support each other as they struggle with the idea that support is possible.

List 11: My Partner's Support Needs

> *physical touch, really be listened to and understood, stable home life, nonjudgmental acceptance, understand needs for outside support, center of your attention, curious rather than critical, explore other's support needs, to be left alone, to be honored and put first, to be given to generously*

Demos

I usually finish the workshop with one or more demonstrations, in which I invite couples to volunteer to work with me in front of the larger group. This further opens participants to the subtleties of the secret language of intimacy—offering the chance to further learn what off-balanced experience and behavior looks like and further witnessing the magic that can take place when couples are given the support they need to identify their underlying yearnings at such times and to explore with each other whether they can find reception.

Because the couples that volunteer for the demos have attended the workshop, which means they have been exploring and learning about their process in an *appreciative* manner and they have become grounded in the support that we have developed together, they are often primed for the adventure of participating in the demos. Undoing what may seem only to be peripheral knots often transforms their experience. With enough such moments in their life, they can transform their ground in such a way that the experience of shame can become a guide to the support needs of both partners, and provide a path to greater connection and belonging on an ongoing basis.

The following are three examples of my working with couples at the end of a workshop that are currently freshest in my mind. Two of the three examples involve same-gendered couples. While this distribution of examples is not representative of the largely heterosexual population that have attended these workshops, as will be seen, these are all stories of human quests for connection that could be found in any couple:

Eva & Alicia

Eva started, sitting a little stiffly, with a guarded look on her face and with a contrasting softness in her eyes, "It seems like we are always busy, with our jobs, the kids, the house.... And lately what time we do have, we seem to bicker with each other. Maybe it's just that we don't have enough time, we're stretched too thin." Alicia, sitting across from Eva and looking a little more relaxed than her partner, replied in a soft tone, "Yes, it hasn't felt good recently."

They both paused and I decided to intervene briefly. I always want my first intervention to reflect something that I sincerely appreciate about the couple.

This is especially true in a workshop demo where the couple has to be aware that all eyes are on them. Thus, I said to them, "Let me get in for just a moment and then I will turn it back to you. The first thing I notice is how important you two are to each other, and I sense a wanting from both of you to connect." I then let them continue.

Alicia spoke next, "We seem to get into this spot from time to time. This last time started for me when I got sick last month. I was really sick." A couple of tears formed and ran slowly down her cheek, and Eva seemed to stiffen a little more. Alicia continued, "You pulled away from me." Eva countered quickly and matter-of-factly, "I'm not sure what you mean; I cooked and brought you food; I took care of the kids; and I took care of the house. Your being sick left me with a lot to do."

What I noticed at this point was an apparent disconnect between Alicia's tears and Eva's stiffening and emotionless voice. So I intervened, asking Eva, "What happens inside of you when you see Alicia's tears?" Eva replied, again matter-of-factly as she grabbed her leg a little tighter, "Well, I see she is hurting, but I want her to understand what her being sick was like for me."

From the nonverbal cues present, it appeared to me that my intervention had hit a pocket of shame, but if it did it also appeared to leave Eva feeling less supported. So I tried again in a compassionate voice, "I'm not sure what I am following here; so bear with me if you can. Is there something about Alicia's tears, or possibly her being sick, that is difficult for you, besides the extra work that her illness caused you?" At this she blurted out, "I can be sick too!" And I said to her, "Could you say a little more about that to Alicia?"

However, Alicia spoke before Eva had a chance to, "I don't understand, I always take care of you when you get sick. And I don't pull away from you." Her voice was concerned, but it appeared that her shame had been activated and that she was becoming defensive. So to support both of them I said to Alicia, "My sense is that Eva has something important to say to you. I know that you have things you want her to hear also, but for now perhaps you could just listen." Eva then spoke, her voice a little harsher, "You don't sit with me." And she started to cry. Alicia replied softly, "Do you mean when you are sick? I always try to do what you would like. I love you." Eva countered, still crying, but with her voice softer this time, "But you don't sit with me." And after a moment she continued, "Do you remember my telling you about when I lived with my aunt after my parents died?" Alicia, now reaching over and holding Eva's hand, said, "Yes, you have told me a lot about that time." Eva continued, crying a little more, "You know that I never felt like my aunt really wanted me, that she was just taking care of me because she felt like she had to." Alicia responded, "Yes, I know." Eva went on, "Well, a time when I would feel that most was when I got sick. My aunt would do all the things that needed to be done to take care of me. Like she would fix and bring me food, but she would not sit with me." At this Eva sobbed even deeper. She continued, "I wanted her so much to sit with me while I ate, but she wouldn't, no matter how much I asked her." Alicia was sitting very close to Eva at this point, holding Eva's hand with both of her own hands while Eva cried. After a bit Alicia said to Eva, "Would you like me to sit with you while you eat when you are sick?" Crying a little less Eva said, "That would feel so good!" Alicia replied, "I can do that."

This vignette illustrates much of what we have covered in this workshop. Although Eva and Alicia had been a committed couple for many of years, Eva had never shared this yearning with her partner.

From our theory we would say that it is highly likely that in response to the trauma of losing her parents and living with an aunt who did not appear to want her, Eva developed ground shame that protected her from exposing her yearning to be sat with when she was sick. (This yearning undoubtedly arose from many sources, including from the grief and loss of belonging associated with losing her parents.) If this is true then anytime that this yearning materialized, she would automatically employ shame to pull her back from exposing or acting on this yearning.

Most recently, this yearning appears to have surfaced and was pulled back when Alicia became sick, which Eva covered by emotionally withdrawing from Alicia and by attempting to go about her life as if nothing mattered. However, her behavior triggered Alicia's shame, which then led to a couple shame cycle, a condition that had lasted for the last month and from which they found themselves bickering with each other—the bickering serving as camouflage for their underlying shamed, unreceived yearnings.

Interestingly enough, they did not need a lot of support from me to undo this knot. My reading the signs of possible shame (learning some of their particular dialect of the secret language of intimacy), such as Eva's becoming stiffer and speaking matter-of-factly (emotionlessly) in response to seeing Alicia's tears, and Alicia becoming defensive when Eva blurted out, "I can be sick too," was the major key to holding them through this process. And with the support I gave them in response to reading those signs, they could do the rest.

Let me emphasize two important factors that contributed to the apparent ease of working with this couple. Again, the effect of couple members exploring and learning about their system in an *appreciative* manner prior to volunteering, and of feeling the connection and support in the group around them, must not be underestimated in opening couples to sharing and being with each other's experience and engaging in this manner. [4]

---

[4] In couples therapy this work would take much longer as the therapist would have to develop the sense of safety and support that is available in

Additionally, understanding what I am attending to in the context of our theory here enables me in situations such as this to do a lot with only a little amount of intervention.

A quick note about my approach in intervening with couples: My intention is always to hold both couple member's struggles simultaneously and to never side with one couple member against the other. That of course is easiest to do when giving system interventions that include both partners. However, I have found that it can be very useful at times to speak solely to one partner or the other. But I am always aware that this carries with it a higher risk of one partner or the other feeling blamed, neglected, or some other variant of shame. So I am always on the lookout for signs of my possible effect on the couple system in this way, and make an effort to repair any such effect when I find that it has occurred.

In this case when Eva stiffened further when I asked her what she felt inside at the sight of Alicia' tears, it appeared to me that I might have shamed her. That is, she might have felt singled out in a negative manner or blamed by my speaking to her individually.

In addition, I was in effect asking Eva to move into the shame she was experiencing in connection with the subject being discussed, which in itself might require additional support from me. My attempt to repair how I might have shamed her and to further support her in tolerating the shame she might be carrying with respect to the situation was to speak more

---

the workshop as well as provide an overall informational framework that can support couples in an appreciative exploration of their system.

compassionately, to tell her something of my intentions, and to invite her to join my exploration. I did all of this by gently saying, "I am not sure what I'm following here; so bear with me if you can." That worked sufficiently so that she could voice more of what she was experiencing.

Eva's subsequent response of "I can be sick too!" was an expression of her underlying shamed yearning. Her word usage and somewhat indignant tone are indicative of what often happens when previously shamed yearnings are first voiced. Such yearnings have been held in place with shame, as they have been considered to be inappropriate. Thus, their first expression will frequently reflect in some manner how they have been held as "not part of our world."

Julia & Kathleen

Julia and Kathleen are a couple in their late twenties who had met in college and who have lived together for the last two years. Julia spoke first. She sat on the edge of her chair, her feet firmly on the ground, her legs angled slightly outward, and her hands on her knees, supporting her upper body in a position of alertness. Her face held a sense of warmth, receptivity and readiness as she said to Kathleen, "What would you like to talk about?" Kathleen also had an air of alertness about her, although she was reclined in her chair with her legs out straight, crossed and resting on the floor. She replied, "I suppose we could talk about the trouble we get into when we try to work together. I mean we do things well a lot, but there are other times that we just seem to get into a knot." Julia agreed, "Yeah, we do get into some snarls don't we." Kathleen proceeded, "The problem is that you just take over and don't let me in."

I could tell that they were warming up quickly, and I already had a hunch about the nature of the knot between them. However, before they went further with trying to understand and possibly getting into their knot, I wanted them to hear something of how I appreciated them. Thus I intervened saying, "Let me get in for a moment, and then you can continue with each other. The first thing that I notice is how bright in spirit you both are. There is an alertness and energy about both of you that I am enjoying." I then let them proceed.

Both appeared to relax a little, and then Kathleen continued where she had left off, "Getting back to what we were talking about, in the current project that we are working on together for the teen center, you just took over when I was working with the first group of kids. I might not have as much experience as you, but I was doing fine." Julia countered, "When the kid's safety is at stake, I can't count on that."

I decided to intervene at this point, saying, "As you two talk about the struggle between you, as to who is in control, I notice how you are sitting, and I wonder if there is a connection. Kathleen, you are sitting in a posture from which I imagine it would be hard to be in control. And Julia, my guess is that it would be difficult to do anything but be in control from the posture that you have chosen. This might just be coincidental, but I wonder what it would feel like to each of you to assume the other person's posture. Would you like to experiment with that a bit?"

I was interested here in whether the postures that they had chosen, which seemed to me to be so pronounced, were indicative of a preferred way they each had of being in the world. And more than that were they also indicative of a taboo (shame) they each felt toward the opposite posture—in other words, was this a complementary polarity? And if this was true, how much awareness did they have of the underlying dynamics it brought them?

They both looked a little confused by what I was asking, but answered me in the affirmative. So I suggested that they both take a good look at how the other person was sitting and then try to assume the other person's posture. As they changed their positions both looked uncomfortable, and in the end neither could duplicate the other's previous posture.

Kathleen was sitting up, but not on the edge of her chair. Her feet were curled in, toward each other, so that they were resting on the outside edges of her soles, in essence not providing much support for her hands and arms. And although her hands were on her knees, her arms were not supporting her upper body. At the same time, while Julia's legs were now stretched out in front of her and her hands were no longer on her knees, she was not leaning back. Her upper body was still supported over her hips, although less well, and she had moved back only slightly from the edge of her chair.

Even with coaching them on what was needed to assume what the other's posture had been, neither could totally do it. I asked them what it felt like to be as close as they were to what the other's posture had been. Both reported that they didn't like being in this position. Kathleen said that she felt "silly," while Julia said her experience was "scary." Of course that was a good indication that we were on the right track.

Normally I would attend to both ends of a complementary polarity in the same experiment. However, Julia appeared to be having much more difficulty than Kathleen in their new positions, so I decided to focus on Kathleen's end of the polarity. I asked her if she would like to experiment a bit more with this position. And she said that she would be willing to do that. So I invited her to lean forward even more toward Julia, perhaps just for an instant, to see what that would feel like. At the same time I asked Julia if that would be OK with her, and she said that it would. With that Kathleen quickly leaned forward, still sitting, toward Julia, and leaned back, to where she had been, just as quickly.

When I asked her what that had been like for her, she said that it was very strange and that she found it embarrassing. Embarrassment indicates the presence of a yearning that one imagines to be inappropriate; so I asked her if she would like to know what it had been like for Julia for her to move closer to Julia in the way she did. Kathleen laughed and said, "she couldn't have liked that, but go ahead. Ask her."

However, Julia didn't wait for my question. She exclaimed to Kathleen, before I could ask, "I loved it! It felt like I really had you for an instant." Kathleen replied in turn, "How could that be? I was so gross." I asked her if she would like to try it again, just to see if she would get the same response from Julia. She acknowledged that she would like to and again leaned forward toward Julia, this time spending a little more time being closer to Julia before leaning back.

Both beamed when Kathleen had leaned forward. So I asked Kathleen what she had seen on Julia's face just then. She replied with a question in her voice, "She looked happy?" Then I asked, "Would you like to hear her say what she experienced?" Upon which Kathleen said to Julia, "How did you like my leaning forward?" And Julia replied, "Oh, darlin', I loved it. Like I said before, I felt like I really got all of you for a time."

I asked Kathleen what she made of Julia's response, and she replied, "I don't know what to make of it. It's very nice, but I am still embarrassed, I'm not sure what to say."

At this point I thought it might be helpful for Kathleen to have a little support with regard to the process of how her original belief around this polarity had formed. So I asked her, "Where did you learn that you shouldn't be forward?" She replied, "Oh, that's no mystery, it has to be from my parents. They were both very stern. Sometimes I felt like if I poked my head out of my shell, it would get knocked off." To which I responded, "So I can appreciate that it is quite a surprise to you that your forwardness would be such a gift to someone. Would you like to share a little more with Julia about your surprise at how much she values this part of you?" Kathleen answered, "Yeah," and to Julia, said, "Are you sure you like this? Can I try it again?" And when Julia replied enthusiastically, "Come on," they played with it a couple more times with similar results.

The couple chose to stop shortly after this and with their permission I then opened the floor, as I usually do following a demo, for participants to ask me about my process during the demo and to share what had been stirred inside them, relating to their own lives, while watching Kathleen and Julia work. In general during this phase, I protect the couple who has worked from answering questions, in respect for the couple's vulnerable position in having just exposed their process and in needing their energy to integrate what just occurred.

After the workshop, Kathleen and Julia approached me and asked if they could have a session with me, and as I had left time on this particular trip to work with people in private sessions before I returned home, we met again a couple of days later.

> After reestablishing my connection with them, I asked Julia and Kathleen what they would like to work on in this session. I noticed they had chosen similar positions to sit as they had at the start of last time, Julia sitting on the edge of her chair, leaning forward, and Kathleen reclined in her chair.
>
> Julia looked at Kathleen, "I don't think I want to do what we were talking about in the car on the way over." Kathleen looked at me and explained with a bit of intensity on her face and in her voice, "I was asking her to work on her vulnerability." I replied to Kathleen, "I am guessing from the tone in your voice that what you say carries some importance to you." Kathleen nodded in agreement. Then to Julia, I said, "And I can appreciate how the subject of one's vulnerability might be a bit scary to anyone." Julia replied, "Yeah, I'm not sure that I want to do that right now."
>
> Several things stood out to me by this time. It appeared to me that they had arrived at the session in a minor couple shame cycle, which had started in the car coming over. My initial intervention here was an attempt to help them unhook from this minor shame

cycle by voicing some part of the message that each was having difficulty getting the other to hear. At the same time, my hope was that this intervention would take me out of the middle, a position of deciding between them in their eyes, by letting them know that I could hear both of their struggles.

I had the sense that what Kathleen was referring to was related to the other side of the polarity that the two of them had worked on last time. One possibility of what happened in the conversation they had in the car was that Kathleen, who had worked on her end of their complementary polarity in the demo, was attempting to equalize their system by asking Julia to work on Julia's end. However, it is also possible that Kathleen was attempting to do that from an off-balanced position (ungrounded sense of herself reflected in her posture, voice tone, and/or word usage) that triggered Julia's sense of needing to be in control. Of course, as Julia had not worked on her end of their polarity as yet, she might not have been able to allow Kathleen to present her concern from a position of balance.

I decided to intervene further. One option would have been to invite them to explore their process during the conversation they had coming over in the car, as it appeared that conversation did not contain enough support for either of them. Following this option could have led in a number of directions including exploring what the nature of the shame knot was for each of them and what support they each might have needed/wanted in order for that conversation to go smoother.

However the same underlying issue might be better addressed by focusing on the other end of their polarity directly. From what happened last time this was one half of the major hidden dynamics in their relationship. Thus if they both wanted to work on the other end of their polarity, it could be very beneficial for them.

I sensed that Julia did have some interest in proceeding along this line. She had used words such as "I think..." and "I'm not sure...," implying ambivalence. My guess was that Julia's resistance to exploring her "vulnerability" was partially the result of the minor couple shame cycle that started in the car prior to the session.

As I had only this session with them before I left town, I decided to see if there was some way to support them in this direction. The challenge was to intervene in a manner that did not increase the shame Julia might be experiencing from their minor couple shame cycle but instead in a way that helped her uncouple from that cycle. I decided to do that by giving her control of the direction we would take.[5]

---

[5] In other situations when I feel strongly about the value of proceeding in a given direction with a couple I might be stronger in

I said to Julia, "I notice that you are sitting in the same posture that you started with last time. I am wondering whether what the two of you are talking about as your "vulnerability" is related to the posture of leaning back that you found scary and couldn't quite do last time." Julia replied, "Maybe.... Yeah, it probably is." I continued, "I could see from last time that was hard for you. And what I think of, in that light, is there is not enough support for you to do that. I wonder... Are you interested in looking into whether we can find sufficient support for you that you would consider exploring what it would feel like to you to lean back? If we don't find sufficient support, then of course, you two should work on something else." Julia replied, cautiously and enquiringly, "OK, but how are you going to do that?"

What I had proposed so far had come from my grounding in our theory here. I didn't have a plan for learning what form the needed support might take. However, as is often the case, when I heard Julia's interest increase, an idea came to me.[6] I shared it

---

advocating for that direction, based on the underlying interest and support that I sense in the couple.

[6] Gestalt theory tells us that we can not know what will happen in the moment until we get there. Additionally, according to the Law of Praegnanz (Koffka, 1935), percepts will find the best organization possible in a given field. Thus it is no surprise that it is difficult for people to be aware of their previously unsupported yearnings or needs until there is sufficient interest and/or other forms of support in the field for these to

with Julia, "What if Kathleen were to lean forward as she did the last time we met? Would you like her to do that, to see if with that you would feel safer?" Julia's voice sounded curious, "Yeah, that would be OK." So I asked Kathleen if she would be willing to do that and she responded enthusiastically that she would like to and leaned forward toward Julia. When I asked Julia how that felt to her, she responded, "Good, but she's got to come even closer." To which Kathleen adjusted her chair and moved closer.

I checked with Julia, "How's that? Does it feel like that gives you enough support to lean back?" Julia, replied, again cautiously, "Yeah, I could try." And she started to lean back toward the back of her chair. Then quickly she said to Kathleen, "You've got to come with me." And Kathleen moved forward, as Julia leaned back until she was resting on the back of her chair. I noted, "This is very interesting, the support that allows you to take the risk of being out of control, is for Kathleen to assume control in a grounded enough manner. Is that right?" Julia replied with a tone that suggested that I was just stating the obvious,

---

emerge. Similarly, it is not uncommon for me to acquire an awareness, of possible meaning and/or a direction in which to proceed, at the moment when it becomes clear there is sufficient support in the field for such an awareness to exist. For this reason I find it important to be curious about and comfortable with what I don't know while attending and to be in tune with and open to the conditions in the field.

"Yeah, of course." I asked Kathleen if she had known this, and she responded in a surprised tone, "No."

In a moment Julia's face softened slightly as a tear ran down her cheek. I asked her what her tear was about, and she said that she didn't know, it just felt scary and strange to be in this position.

At this point I wanted to make sure that Julia was feeling sufficient support. I asked her, "Do you sense that Kathleen is with you?" Julia responded, "Yeah, she's there. I feel like I have her." I continued, "How are you doing? Are you OK?" And Julia answered, a little jokingly "Well, I'm not real comfortable with this." And then in a slightly softer voice, "But I am OK."

Julia's tears continued to slowly form and run down her cheek. I thought it might help Julia to have a better sense of the history of the polarity that she was dealing with. So I asked her, "I am guessing that you learned some place that you needed to be the one in charge—that you didn't have anyone else that you could count on. Is that true?" Julia's voice intensified, "Are you kidding? My family was so chaotic. I couldn't count on anyone. I remember at four years old I took my bike apart, fixed it, and put it back together because there was no one else that would do it for me or with me." I replied, "So if you're not in charge things don't get done." Julia confirmed, "You got it!" I continued, "It sounds like you have been alone with this for a long time." Julia's tears came quicker, and she said more softly, "Yeah." At the same time her face softened substantially as she continued to look into Kathleen's face.

For the rest of the session I helped them stay with this intersubjective moment, exploring their experience and getting feedback from one another as to the importance that this way of being with each other held for both of them.

The above vignette is an illuminating example of unawares complementarity in a couple system and of the individual and couple shame cycles that can ensue in such cases. It reflects the transformations that can occur when couple members' shame is followed with sufficient support and an opportunity becomes possible for couple members to expose/discover their underlying yearnings and to explore whether these yearnings can find connection. Again the power of a workshop that approaches participants in this manner, in supporting couples to take such risks, must not be underestimated.

As Gestalt theory predicts, the catalyst for transforming couple members' belief systems is new intersubjective experience (contact) in which they can test out and learn that their underlying yearnings are valued and can be received. Thus I facilitate, support, and stay with such intersubjective experience whenever possible. Each step in the sequenced layering of response following response, in which couple members express their yearning for and/or their reception of their partner (encapsulated in their posture, gestures, facial expression, voice tone, word usage, tears, sighs, and other verbal and nonverbal expressions), contains a wealth of material that is invaluable (for both the couple and the therapist) in helping couples redefine their sense of what is "our world" and what is not. Such redefinition of previously shamed yearnings from "not our world" to "our world" requires staying with this intersubjective process from step to step, noticing/attending to shame experiences that could derail the process as they materialize along the way, and helping couple connections emerge, develop, and become fully recognized. Of course, "birthing" voices and new ways of connecting in this manner means that couple members will experience some shame in the form of shyness, embarrassment, feeling "silly," "stupid," "awkward," "selfish," or the like, during this process. A wonderful aspect in working with couples is that they often have potential resources in this regard that they don't understand or know how to access.

This vignette reflects the risk of focusing on just one end of a complementary polarity in a demo situation. Kathleen and Julia's system did appear to be unbalanced slightly because the two of them solely worked on Kathleen's end of their complementary polarity in the demo—witness their apparent minor couple shame cycle in the car driving to the second session. However, it appeared from the information gained in both sessions that Julia was too vulnerable in the face of giving up the protection of her end of this polarity, and would not have been able to work on her associated taboo until Kathleen had first taken a step in owning the value of her own forwardness. In retrospect, to support this couple better at the end of the demo, I would have liked to have given them a cautionary note on what they might encounter because they had only worked on one end of their complementary polarity

Wayne & Beth

Wayne and Beth, a couple in their early 40s, have been married a number of years. Beth, sitting in a relaxed but alert fashion opposite her husband, started, "I want to thank you for having the courage to come today. I know counseling is my thing, not yours. So I just want you to know that I appreciate you doing this." Wayne responded with a softness both on his face and in the way he was sitting, "I have to say I am scared—partially just because of being here and partially because I have something that I want to tell you. I'm sorry that you've had to put up with my behavior over the years. I haven't known how to be more responsible and not let it get on you."

This couple had very quickly entered an area that appeared to have great significance for them. I wanted them to hear something about how I appreciated their process before I intervened in another way; so I said to them, "Let me get in for an instant and then you can resume. I am appreciative of how sweetly you are talking to each other and how much you are trying to understand each other's experience." With that I turned it back to them.

Wayne turned back to Beth and continued what he had been saying, "I have a black box inside of me that

I fall into, and when I do I want to be better at separating myself and taking care of it. I haven't been so good at doing that in the past." Beth replied, also with a soft tone, "The biggest problem for me is that you separate yourself. You just disappear, and I can't reach you." Wayne countered with his voice still soft but much firmer, "But I have to. That is my responsibility. I have to take care of it myself."

I intervened here, saying to Wayne, "I just want to clarify something. It sounds to me from what you are saying and the caring way that you are saying it that you are trying to protect Beth. Is that right?" Wayne replied, "Yeah, this shouldn't get on her." Then to Beth I said, "Did you understand that his intent was to protect you?" She answered, "Sometimes I can get there, but mostly I just feel shut out." And then to Wayne she said, "You don't need to protect me; I want to be with you at those times." Wayne answered her, "No, you don't know how horrible it is. I can't let this get on you." Tears formed in his eyes. He shifted his posture slightly, placing his hand on his stomach.

I intervened at this point, saying to Wayne, "Could you tell Beth what your tears are about?" Wayne replied, "What happens to me when I fall into my black box is just disgusting. I don't want it to get on you." Beth replied, "But I would like to be with you." Wayne answered, "No, that's not right."

I intervened again addressing Wayne, "I hear that you are repulsed by how you feel when you are in your black box. I also hear that you expect Beth to be as repulsed as you are. What if she is not? Have you really checked that out?" His tears started to slowly flow, and he said, "How could she not be disgusted?" I answered, "Well, I am wondering if part of your disgust comes from the situation in which you learned that you had to be alone with what you experience at these times. I'm guessing that was a long time ago. Do you remember when that was?" Wayne replied, "That must have been around what happened with my father." And Beth volunteered, "His father was very physically abusive with him."

I continued, "Maybe Beth is different from the people around you when you learned that you needed to be alone. I'm guessing that there was some reason why you picked her. Would you like to experiment with that just a little?" Wayne replied, "What do you mean?" I answered, "Perhaps you could tell her just a little more of what your experience is like when you are in your black box and see how she responds." At this Wayne said, "I really don't know how to describe it."

At this point I thought that Wayne might be supported better with more contact with his sensations. I was guessing that his hand, resting on his stomach, was touching the place where he experienced the sensations he associated with his black box. However, I didn't want to just yet risk interfering with his self support by focusing on the placement of his hand, so I asked him, "Where in your body is your black box located?" Wayne thought only an instant and replied, tapping his stomach with his hand, "Right here." And I said, "Could you tell Beth a little of what you feel there?" Wayne replied, "I don't know what to say. It's just like a vast emptiness. But I can't describe it more than that. Very threatening." I asked him if he would like to hear Beth's reaction to what he had reported, and he said he would. Beth offered without my asking, "I'm fine. I don't feel any disgust. I just feel grateful that you are telling me."

I asked Wayne what he made of what Beth had said. And he replied, "I don't understand it. I didn't say much. But I don't know how to say more."

Wayne's tone had changed. It looked to me like Wayne might be feeling enough support to go a little deeper. Perhaps now I could focus on his hand placement. There was a good chance that there was some kind of longing there. So I said to him, "I notice that your hand is on the spot where you say your black box is located. I imagine you have it there because it feels comfortable to do so." Wayne replied, "I hadn't thought of it. But yes I guess it does." I continued, "I wonder... Would you like to experiment a little further and see what it would feel like for Beth to place her hand on that spot?" He replied, "I'm not sure." And then after a short pause he continued, "Maybe I could put my hand on her stomach." And I responded, "That too. Would you like to ask her if she would like to do that?" Wayne asked Beth and she said that she would like to do that; so they shifted their chairs so that they could get close enough. Once Beth placed her hand on Wayne's stomach and he placed his hand on her stomach, both of their bodies relaxed. I let them sit there for a moment.

After a bit, I checked with Wayne, "How are you doing; are you OK with this?" He replied that he was OK. I then asked him if he could take Beth with him inside his black box. He replied as a tear rolled down his face, "She's already there." I asked him what that was like, and he responded, "Less lonely," and more tears formed and flowed down his cheek.

This was clearly a moment of intimate connection for both of them, and I let them just be with it for a while. I then asked Wayne if he had anything he wanted to share with Beth about his experience, and he said to Beth, "I don't know what to say, it just feels less lonely." Likewise, I asked Beth if there was anything that she wanted to share with Wayne about her experience now. And she said to Wayne, "This feels very good. I am so happy that you let me be with you." Again, I let them sit with their experience.

This moment seemed to be complete for them so I asked them if they wanted to stop here, and they both said yes. I then asked Wayne if he felt like this was a position that he could assume again some time with Beth, at the same time asking Beth if she would like that. Both said that they would like to do it again. So I suggested that they experiment with this position from time to time.

Beth ended the session with saying to Wayne, "Before we stop, I just want you to know again how thankful I am that you had the courage to do this. And I want you to know that you aren't the only one that has a black box between us. I have one too. And I want you to come visit mine as well."

Again in this deceptively simple demo, this workshop facilitated this couple taking quite a large step in finding a connection for which they both had longed, on some level, for many years. The process of undoing their knot in the demo started with my hearing Wayne's intent to protect Beth by trying to handle his experience by himself.

A common additional layering of shame can occur in relational interactions when the effect of one person's behavior toward the other is different from the intent. Both the intent and the effect can become sources of shame that can trigger a couple shame cycle. In this case, Wayne could be shamed because his intent to protect was not being received by Beth. On the other hand Beth could be shamed both around her yearning to be with her husband when he separated himself from her and around her intent to take care of him when that happened, which was not received by Wayne.

Of course this knot was complicated by the hidden element that what Wayne was trying to protect Beth from was how repulsive he thought he was when he experienced the feelings he associated with his black box. Since his shame prevented him from sharing his sense of being repulsive, he could not test out whether Beth likewise found him to be repulsive.

Wrapping Up

There are many ingredients that underpin the success of this workshop. They include learning about the existence of shame —a hidden regulator of couple interactions—as an attempt to protect, as information about our perceived condition of our larger field, and as an indication of an underlying yearning for connection. They also include learning about the intricacies and complexities of shame-controlled couple interactions and most importantly learning that the antidote for shame is support and connection. And equally importantly they include having all this occur through a safe enough experiential basis in which participants can obtain a felt sense of how this applies to their own lives.

The feedback from participants following this workshop has been heartwarming. It includes numerous instances of couples sharing that they have rediscovered their love for one another. It also includes accounts of individual experiences such as a woman reporting that following the workshop she had recurrent dreams that her shame was of a frozen crystalline structure which a new light was melting. In general the feedback reflects a sense that participants have become more aware of their and their partner's shame, feel less alone in the experience of their shame, and have either gained an experience of or have some sense of the possibility of an ensuing deeper bond with their partner. Such is the paradoxical nature of the secret language of intimacy.

References for Chapters 1-5

Balcom, D., Lee, R. G., & Tager, J. (1995). The systemic treatment of shame in couples. *Journal of Marital and Family Therapy*, *21*(1), 55-65.

Darwin, C. (1872). *The Expression of the Emotions in Man and Animals*. London: John Murray.

Gottman, J. (1994). *Why Marriages Succeed or Fail*. New York: Simon & Schuster.

Kofka, K. (1935). *Principles of Gestalt Psychology*. New York: Harcourt, Brace, & World, Inc.

Kaufman, G. (1980). *Shame: The Power of Caring*. Rochester VT: Shenckman.

Kaufman, G. (1989). *The Psychology of Shame*. New York: Springer Publishing Co.

Lee, R. G. (Ed.) (2004a). *The Values of Connection: A Relational Approach to Ethics*. Hillsdale, NJ: GestaltPress/The Analytic Press.

Lee, R. G. (2004b). Working with couples: Application of Gestalt's values of connection. In R. G. Lee (Ed.), *The Values of Connection: A Relational Approach to Ethics* (pp. 159-177). Hillsdale, NJ: GestaltPress /The Analytic Press.

Lee, R. G. (2002). Ethics: A gestalt of values/The values of Gestalt. *The Gestalt Review*, 6(1), 27-51.

Lee, R. G. (2001). Shame & support: Understanding an adolescent's family field. In M. McConville & G. Wheeler (Eds.). *Heart of Development: Gestalt Approaches to Working with Children and*

Adolescents. Vol II - Adolescents (pp. 253-270). Hillsdale, NJ: Analytic Press.

Lee, R. G. (1996). The waif and Mr. Hyde. In R. G. Lee & G. Wheeler (Eds.), *The Voice of Shame: Silence and Connection in Psychotherapy* (pp. 177-201). San Francisco: Jossey-Bass.

Lee, R. G. (1995). Gestalt and shame: The foundation for a clearer understanding of field dynamics. *The British Gestalt Journal*, 4(1), 14-22.

Lee, R. G. (1994a). Couples' shame: The unaddressed issue. In G. Wheeler & S. Backman (Eds.), *On Intimate Ground: A Gestalt Approach to Working with Couples* (pp. 262-290). San Francisco: Jossey-Bass.

Lee, R. G. (1994b). The effect of internalized shame on marital intimacy. (Unpublished doctoral dissertation, Fielding Institute, Santa Barbara, CA.)

Lee, R. G., & Wheeler, G. (Eds.). (1996). *The Voice of Shame: Silence and Connection in Psychotherapy*. San Francisco, Jossey-Bass.

Lewis, H. B. (1971). *Shame and Guilt in Neurosis*. New York: International Universities Press.

Nathanson, D. L. (1987). Shaming systems in couples, families and institutions. In D. L. Nathanson (Ed.), *The Many Faces of Shame* (pp. 246-271). New York: Guilford Press.

Retzinger, S. M. (1987). Resentment and laughter: Video studies of the shame-rage spiral. In H. B. Lewis (Ed.). *The Role of Shame in Symptom Formation* (pp. 151-181). Hillsdale, NJ: Lawrence Erlbaum Associates, Publishers.

Siegel, D. J. (1999). *The Developing Mind: How Relationships and the Brain Interact to Shape Who We Are*. New York: The Guilford Press.

Stern, D. N. and the Boston Change Process Study Group (2003). On the other side of the moon: The importance of implicit knowledge for Gestalt therapy. In M. Spagnuolo Lobb & N. Amendth-Lyons (Eds.), *Creative License: The Art of Gestalt Therapy*, (pp.). New York: Springer.

Stern, D. (1977). *The First Relationship*. Cambridge, MA: Harvard University. Press.

Taylor, C. (1992). *The Ethics of Authenticity*. Cambridge, MA: Harvard University Press.

Tomkins, S. S. (1963). *Affect, Imagery, and Consciousness: The Negative Affects*, (Vol. 2). New York: Springer.

Wheeler, G. (1996). Self and shame: a new paradigm for psychotherapy. In R. Lee & G. Wheeler (Eds.). *The Voice of Shame: Silence and Connection in Psychotherapy* (pp. 23-58). San Francisco: Jossey-Bass.

Wheeler, G. (2000). *Beyond Individualism: Toward a New Understanding of Self, Relationship, & Experience*. Hillsdale, NJ: The Analytic Press/GestaltPress.

Wheeler, G. (2004). Shame and belonging: Homer's *Iliad* and the Western ethical tradition. In R. G. Lee (Ed.), *The Values of Connection: A Relational Approach to Ethics* (pp. 283-309). Hillsdale, NJ: GestaltPress/The Analytic Press.

Zinker, J. C. (1983), Complementarity and the middle ground in couples, *The Gestalt Journal* 6(2), 13-27.

Part II

••••••••

Contributors' Essays

Editor's Note:

In the following chapter, Margherita Spagnuolo Lobb sensitively, eloquently, and with intellectual acumen explores the process of meeting an intimate other, an experience which is among the most delicate and most sought after of all human endeavors, and which is the heart of every couple relationship. She captures the strength of the yearning, the risk of humiliation, the interruption of intention, and the resulting loss of spontaneity that can so easily occur in this process. We are permitted a view of a master therapist and trainer as she holds and supports couples to take needed risks in recovering their spontaneous creativity.

6

•••••••••••

Being at the Contact
Boundary with the Other:
The Challenge of Every Couple

Margherita Spagnuolo Lobb

On an unquiet beach,
a man and a woman were walking
and the vast shadow of a dilemma lay on them

… It was the usual dilemma,
an elementary dilemma:
whether their love made sense or not.

… The dilemma represents
the balance of the forces in the field,
because loving and fighting
are the shapes of our time.

(from *Il dilemma*, Giorgio Gaber)

Robert Lee's contribution on couples vividly provides a concrete language—the concept of shame as a relational experience as opposed to the experience of "feeling at home" with the partner—that can easily become a tool for couples to understand what happens between them in positive and creative terms. I was left so touched and deeply supported by the reading of his contribution, that I finally defined it as a growth experience. Reading it was useful for me even with regard to my own couple relationship—it opened my heart and mind to the experience of my partner. It really helped me to not cling to my wounds, while waiting for them to heal, but rather to attend to the wounds of the other. And as a psychotherapist, it helped me to instantly grasp that the most profound aid that any therapy can give to a couple in a critical moment is precisely the ability to open up to the other.

The profound awareness of being a couple, of being two, implies being interested in the other as other, as novelty, besides our perception of the other, which rather frames and triggers our fear that we will not be accepted, or our fear of having to stop on our way towards the significant other.

Hence this book presents a perspective as well as a professional tool that is near to human experience, one that further enriches the original methodological contribution made by Gestalt therapy to psychotherapeutic work with couples. In an extraordinarily phenomenological perspective, this approach is based on the assumption that it is from the experience co-created by the partners, through their interacting with each other, that change emerges, and not from modifications of the systems which are offered by the psychotherapist(s).

What could I add to such an informed, skilled, touching,

profound therapeutic tool for couples? Within the same procedural frame of reference, from my experience as a therapist and as a long-time member of a couple (25 years), I will provide: 1) an introduction to the specificity of Gestalt therapy with couples, and three dimensions of the experience of couples to notice and to welcome each other, entitled respectively: 2) whom do we live with? 3) what keeps us linked? and 4) we fight as a way to fill the relational void. I will finish with a section entitled: 5) what does a therapist do who believes in the value of spontaneity in couple systems?

Gestalt therapy:
The life of couples as excitement and growth
at the contact boundary

The book which marked the birth of Gestalt therapy (Perls et al., 1951/1994) offers a central idea, stressed by the subtitle— "(Novelty), Excitement and Growth in the Human Personality"—which is fundamental for the life of the couple. The spontaneous human ability to be fully present (that is, with the senses awakened) at the contact boundary with the environment[1] is shaped for the couple in the ability to maintain the spontaneity of seeing, feeling attracted, allowing oneself to be changed, by the other, precisely as *other*, by the other we do not expect, by the other as novelty. It is not easy for adults to

---

[1]For a detailed definition of the terms "contact," "contact boundary," "awareness," "self," and "functions of the self," see Spagnuolo Lobb, 2005a; 2001; 2004; 2005b.

achieve this quality of the dialogic encounter, because stripping oneself of the fear of reopening old wounds demands genuine training. But it is only if we are "naked" before the other, if we are fully present in the here and now with the other, that it is possible to support the evolution of the excitement[2] of the encounter. To reach this goal, we must recognize our own fears (and the objections which, in consequence, we develop towards the other) which clothe the most intimate part of our person; and we must also recognize the experience of the other.

When we reach that point, we can tune in to our own and the other's intentionality of contact. The more the partners meet in the fullness of their senses, the more they are aware of the totality of the experience they co-create when they meet, the more the regulation that occurs at the contact boundary between the two is "therapeutic," in that it opens the fullness of intimacy to both. Hence couple members need to have, as a normal condition, the ability to perceive their contact boundary (the I and the you in the act of meeting) clearly, with all the senses awakened.

Being a couple takes us into the dimension not only of intimacy, but also of our radically being social animals (Kitzler, 2003; Bloom, 2003). Many of today's psychological theories agree that we construct ourselves in interaction with the environment, both human and non-human (Searles, 1960).

---

[2] The term "excitement" includes the sense of psycho-physical energy and of intentionality in entering into contact with the other. It thus integrates at a phenomenological level the experience as lived in the body and at the same time oriented to the encounter with the other.

Infant research has shown how social abilities develop in the child literally from birth (the child is "programmed" for this). The so-called "intersubjective" islands (Stern, 2004; Beebe & Lachmann, 2002) between child and caregivers are the first places in which is formed the self-in-contact, the individual's way of being-with. These intersubjective abilities are for the child the ground of the experience of intimacy, on which rests the sense of personal security and flexibility in accepting the new—the creative adjustment to the environment (Perls et al., 1951/1994). The caregiver-child dyad is self-regulating and the child learns ways, rather than contents, of being with the other. The rhythm, co-created by the caregiver-child dyad, between excitement and acceptance, processes and contents, forms a dance, an experiential code that the child learns. It is precisely this code that the adult uses, in both intimate and social relationships. S/he tends to recreate ways of being-with—s/he will expect certain reactions of the other and will usually see what s/he is used to seeing. Daniel Stern and the Boston Change Process Study Group (Stern et al., 1998a, 1998b; Stern, 2004) call this experiential code "implicit knowledge" and consider it fundamental to meaningful relationships, including the one between therapist and client. I believe that implicit knowledge is also what gives shape to the couple's dynamic. It is the focus on which successful psychological help is centered, regardless of theoretical orientation (Stern, 2000).

We are beings-in-relation, and this contemporary perspective on the centrality of the relationship makes the couple of outstanding interest for the world of psychology and psychotherapy. Whereas many approaches conceived for the study of the individual are opening up today to interesting perspectives on relationship, Gestalt therapy remains incredibly original in its initial intuition of the experience that occurs at the contact boundary, in the "between" the I and the you. Couple relationship is thus seen by Gestalt therapy as a continuous co-creation of the contact boundary, as an experience that arises or builds a history in the space that lies "between" the partners, not as a projection on to the other of personal experiences. The relational dimension comes before the internal dimension, or at least *cannot be explained from the experience of the individual.*

The life of the couple is a relational improvisation (Spagnuolo Lobb, 2003) that encloses the most profound dimension of social life. This transports the couple beyond the strategic attitude of the social ego which in effect teaches us solitude. It is our relational patterns of intimacy which hold our abilities to be group animals.

Whom do we live with?

I wish you would smoke me with
as much pleasure as you smoke
cigarettes.

I wish you'd decide to relax with
me the way you do with them.

Smoking is a surrogate for a
shared pleasure: that's why it's
harmful.

It's a retroflected pleasure.
The real pleasure for which we're
made, the one that makes your
self-awareness expand
marvelously,

is the pleasure we find neither in
ourselves nor in the other, but at
the boundary,

in that space which is neither in
us nor in the other:

it's at the point where we meet.

It's the pleasure we can derive
from the profound psycho-
physical encounter with another
person.

Unfortunately, it's also the
pleasure that frightens us most.

That's why I wish you would
smoke me as you smoke
cigarettes.

(from a client's letter to her lover)

With its theory of self as a process of contact making and withdrawal, Gestalt therapy invites us to look at how couples realize or avoid their intentionality to reach and be reached by the other. So, I focus here mainly on how couples interrupt their intentionality for contact, thus losing their spontaneity, and how instead they interact with creative adjustment. Feelings such as shame, anger, love, and belongingness, are basic elements of this process.

The following is an example of incomprehension in a couple, based on a wish to take care of the other where the other is not seen as "other."

Rita and Gianni have been married for 27 years. Gianni is a businessman, often stressed because of the financial risks inherent in his job. He usually likes to deal with moments of anxiety by enjoying the pleasures of life. Two of his favorite pleasures, in this regard, are eating and smoking.

Rita is a teacher; she's a very feisty, energetic woman. Conversely, for her the pleasures of life are a form of weakness that cannot be yielded to when there is a problem to be solved.

They are both very generous and capable of making great sacrifices for each other, but not so good at looking after themselves. Gianni's job conditions their life as a couple to a considerable extent. He does not conceal the tensions he experiences and has to manage and Rita, worried about her husband's stress, tries to keep him in good physical shape.

A typical situation in which these dynamics play a significant role frequently occurs when Gianni comes home from work worried about what is going to happen the following day (for example, whether he will be able to re-sell the goods he has bought, or whether the banks will permit him a loan, all possibilities that will affect his own and his family's wellbeing). He'd like to relax and finally devote himself to some of the pleasures of life. So he eats everything on the table with gusto, and if there are strawberries and cream he shovels them down as if there was nothing else in his stomach, or he goes out on the balcony to enjoy a smoke.

What he finds relaxing is cause for great anxiety for Rita. Concerned that her husband is under so much stress at work, she tries to protect him from further fatigue caused by food or the toxic nature of smoking. Convinced that her solution is the only healthy (and indeed the most reasonable) thing her husband can do, and without wondering whether his experience may be different, Rita starts removing the food from Gianni's view, while reminding him not to smoke because it's bad for him.

Gianni, who is just beginning to unwind and leave the stress of the office behind, experiences his wife's recommendations as thrusting him back into a state of stress. His sense of relaxation evaporates in the face of having to submit to the wishes and anxiety of another person, and he is seized by anger.

Since he is a kindly person (he's inclined to retroflect his anger), he doesn't shout, but asks his wife to let him do as he pleases, and eats even more, in the hope of rediscovering the pleasure linked to food. But by this point his wife has ruined it for him, and he ends up eating not because he's hungry but partly to show his wife that she doesn't make decisions for him, and partly to rediscover the relaxation he so longs for. He gets angry because she decides for him, and his eating too much in spite of her warnings is equivalent to telling her: "I'm the one who makes the decisions."

She certainly shows a lack of faith in his ability to self-regulate. However, ironically, this is linked to the conflictual attitude she has towards her own ability to be a grown-up and to help. Rita is the youngest of four sisters, all at least ten years older than she. She's always been the baby of the household, and has not developed much security in her ability to take care of others. So she looks over her husband with all the worry of a child who wants to help in a difficult situation, but has little sense that she will be received as a grown up and, accordingly, acts with little skill or grace. She feels this anxiety when she sees him, a grown-up, in difficulty, and attempts to help in a manner that, while being well intentioned, caring, and insightfully directed, is also cold, without affection, and which he experiences as castrating.

There is an additional experience configuring his response. He is the second of two brothers. Together he and his brother have bought out their father's business. He has been the brother who works in silence, who has to submit to the "grown-ups" (his older brother's, and his father's) decisions. Having to accept decisions he did not agree with, he has experienced the humiliation of not being considered. He never felt that the other males in the family (his father and brother) noticed his devoted contribution. Now, every time that a decision is made without taking into account his point of view, he feels unseen, humiliated, and angry. And he reacts strongly, even imposingly, although usually indirectly and retroflectively (turning his energy back against himself), in an attempt to gain a sense that his wishes will be heard.

The main stress of his relationships is therefore the stress of having to fight for the right to even have desires, and a sense of the world, that are different from others'. When his wife imposes herself so insistently, and controls his life by emptying the fridge, and cooking nothing but vegetables (for his good), he relives the stress of others' past impositions, grows silently angry and takes up the battle to make his desires count. Thus, what usually begins as a wish to take care of the other (on her part) and to relax in intimate conditions (on his part), always ends up in a fight against the person making decisions on his behalf (for him) and in the despair of being unable to help (for her).

What keeps us linked?

Work like you don't need the money.
Love like you've never been hurt.
And dance like nobody is watching.

S. Clark & R. Leigh

Both partners in a couple are motivated by two factors in their interaction—the intentionality of contact, of reaching the other, and the fear that this intention is not understood by the other. The movement towards the significant other—like any sort of open exposure—lays the partners bare to the risk of humiliation, of being negatively evaluated as if they were doing something wrong. This is where I locate shame—in the process of projecting on to the other the lack of understanding which was previously experienced in a meaningful relational field. *What hurts is not so much not being understood by the other in the content of our experience, but rather in our desire and our attempts to reach the other, in our wish for meaningful contact, for an intimate sharing.* It is rather like the experience of feeling that we are being laughed at when we are naked.

As couple members, our core longing is to show our self and to see the other in the nakedness of the immediate experience. This is our need for intimacy, which is sought as a feeling of being at home, as the relaxation a child experiences in its mother's arms, as the recognition that the traveler feels in body and soul on finally returning home. The other is desired as an accepting body, a home in which to take shelter from bad weather, the world where you can speak your own language.

The way this desire is experienced and expressed in the couple can be saturated with fears that the other will not be where we want to find her/him, that the other will be, metaphorically, elsewhere. Thus, longing for the other in this manner, beyond the moment of falling in love which is by definition blind, may also be felt as an intense risk that the desire for intimacy will be frustrated, that there will be a repetition of previous failures in one's meaningful relationships. In this way, engaging the other is also risking finding the outsider who doesn't understand, finding unsafe arms (fear of which keeps our body alert), and/or finding the noisy home where it is impossible to rest.

So fear and risk, as Laura Perls (cf. Bloom, 2005) used to say, create the special vibration that is characteristic of the tension towards the other in a couple. Every meaningful interaction of the couple, like the entire life of the couple, is a story with—we hope—a happy ending: one in which the process of our meaningful relationships is remade, in which we experience our renewed, increased ability to contact the other in full awareness, really seeing the other, beyond the projections of rejection, and thus being able to fulfill our desire to reach the other.

These dynamics may take place in any valued, close relationship, not solely with couples that are married or cohabiting. For example, a good illustration of them occurred between two co-therapists who came to me for supervision.

Although they are not a couple in private life, Michela and Filippo have been working together for 15 years. They have run groups and family therapy sessions together since the beginning of their professional lives. They began working in a cultural context where psychotherapy was practically unknown; so, if on the one hand working together allowed them to support each other, on the other choosing each other was in a sense "dictated by necessity."

They are very different in character and there is something magical about the fact that they have never told each other to go to hell. Their very differentness has made them appreciated by the couples and groups with whom they work—when a patient or a member of a group feels that Michela doesn't understand her, she most often feels at home with Filippo and vice versa.

Although not a couple in private life, the dynamics between them and the relational field they create are typical of a couple in constant conflict. Obviously, the job they do helps them to take the best out of their relationship and keeps them from being destroyed by the wounds which they, involuntarily and continually, inflict on each other.

They ask for a session because they are having great difficulty in sharing anything outside the sessions they run with clients. This creates a climate of stress between them and limits their therapeutic potential. Indeed, both of them have the impression that whenever they open up to the other, the other reacts unfailingly with unexpected anger or cynical sarcasm, causing bitterness and a closing down by the one who has taken the risk of being open.

> I ask Michela: Can you describe what happens in these cases?
>
> Michela: Yes, I remember a week ago. We'd run a group in a way that was harmonious and profitable for the participants. The atmosphere between us while we were with the group was so great that I'd relaxed, and when we were on our own saying goodbye, I quite spontaneously told him something I hadn't told him before, hoping to clear up what I hadn't understood about him.
>
> Therapist: What exactly did you tell him?
>
> Michela: Well... I don't remember now, I guess it isn't important...
>
> Filippo interrupts: I do remember, and what do you mean it isn't important! You throw rocks and then run away! You told me I'd been irresponsible when I didn't take a position against the owner of the office who wanted to raise the rent. It was like a bolt from the blue, a real blow that I wasn't expecting in such a harmonious atmosphere.
>
> Noticing that Michela is holding her breath and closing up, I ask her: Apparently your intentionality wasn't what Filippo understood.

So what was the message that you wanted him to hear?

Michela: Yeah, that's always the way between us: every time I try to understand him, he interprets it as an attack. I just wanted to understand why on earth he had behaved in a way that I thought was irresponsible. I wasn't making a value judgment. I was communicating my emotion. And it's because I really don't think he's irresponsible that I want to understand how to read his behavior.

Filippo, obviously agitated: Sure, you're so good at using the subtleties of the job. I'm not a fool, and it's quite clear to me that you want to use a quibbling communication technique to cover up what you really think of me. You think I'm irresponsible and you're the only one who's any good.

The situation seems to be in jeopardy, and to stay within the bounds of the task the couple has given me, I support them so that they can get back to the intentionality of reaching one another.

I ask: What do you feel, Michela, at this point, and you, Filippo, at this point, and what would you each have liked to accomplish with the other, with which you now feel disappointed?

Michela: At the moment when I raised this business of the rent, I'd like to have understood in what way you, Filippo, *are not* irresponsible as you seem to be to me. Maybe I'm being judgmental, projective, as you say, but at that moment it was my way of opening the door to you, calling into question the wounds that my perception of you causes. Your angry reaction made me close up again. I'm sorry I ever opened that door. I'm sorry I can't contact you.

Filippo: That day with the group had really been great. For me it seemed like an almost impossible dream to be able to work with you that way. I expected that atmosphere to remain while we were saying goodbye. I'd have liked to thank you for the way you'd been with me, but I felt that I'd been pushed under a cold shower. It was so unexpected and painful that in my blind despair I thought you were doing it on purpose, that you'd been giving the impression of being nice to me just so that you could stab me all the more fiercely and cruelly. Yes, at times like that I think you enjoy hurting me. I wanted to feel relaxed with you, and instead I had to suddenly defend myself against a cruel attack.

As a therapist, it seems to me that at this moment, when the wounds are opening, support may be useful to differentiate the old relational experiences that each of the pair tends to repeat from what their relationship can become, free of painful projections.

So I remark: At these times when you are hoping to finally reach the other, you each have the impression that the other is doing something that makes you draw back into yourselves, disappointed. It seems that at these times a relational destiny is fulfilled, and the attempt to contact each other in the intimacy you would like comes to a bitter conclusion. What is it that you'd like to find in each other?

Michela answers: My father used to get really angry sometimes with my mother. When my mother would ask him for something for herself, he'd shout and look offended. That would frighten me and I'd make myself small. I'd have liked to defend my mother, but I didn't actually do it. I've always wanted to find in you, Filippo, the desire to answer my questions, rather than anger and taking offence because you're not understood.

Filippo answers: My mother would seduce me with her love, and then the next minute she'd turn on me. I never knew how long the peaceful moments would last, because the storm would arrive unexpectedly. I could never forecast it and above all I felt profoundly devalued in my longing for peace and love by her crazy unpredictability. The most reasonable thing I could think of if I didn't want to believe she was crazy was that she was doing it on purpose, that she enjoyed hurting me. I've always wanted to trust you, Michela, to feel that you were steady, logical.

Michela looks at him sadly and says: I'm sorry my attempts to understand you better strike you as attacks or even worse, as unforeseen storms. I feel close to you and I'd like you to feel that my questions are just a wish to get to know you better, not attacks.

Filippo, letting out a long breath, says: I'm sorry that my attempts to defend myself, which you feel as violent, make you draw back. I like the fact that you're curious about me and I'd like you not to close up, to go on wanting to get to know me in spite of everything.

In this example, recognizing the experience of the other in her/his differentness and at the same time in her/his interweaving with their individual and joint fears has led to a differentiated perception of the other and of the relational patterns. This process has helped Michela and Filippo to reach each other. The risks they have taken have received the needed support to drive their interaction to the desired intimacy.

We fight as a way to fill the relational void

I am
- in your arms -
tasting the fragility
of this relationship.

For the first time
feeling you to be
different from what I would like
makes me feel
the sweet vibrant sense of reality.

I wish there were no longer
the dream of what is not:
that is what enables
not being there.

But being with the only
fragile presence I have
is new, disappointing
and true at the same time,
incredibly strong
in its fragility.

Following the intentionality of contact demands an initial disintegration of the self, of one's own certainties, to strip oneself before the novelty represented by the other. This instant of nakedness is delicate, it often becomes filled with past pains, often not consciously perceived, but perceived instead as evidence of a negative intention on the part of the other. The wicked other (paranoid experience) or the other who wants to cheat (borderline experience), or is too small, needing our help and incapable of containing us (narcissistic experience), fills the void into which we fling ourselves when we dare to open again the possibility of offering ourselves in a meaningful contact, where we hope it is possible to find the intimacy we desire. It is simply safer to stay on known ground.

While (re)cognizing the other's motivations as typical of her/his way of reacting, and not linked to a lack of understanding or of interest towards us, we fail to take the new step—for instance, we don't apologize when we understand that we have offended the other, we don't smile although we know that smiling would be the solution to a quarrel, we simply remain in old patterns of behavior, out of plain fear of changing, despite the fact that our perception of the other has changed.

This kind of quarrel is often seen in long-standing couples, in whom the habit of not feeling understood has become "encysted" and, although the partners have developed good life-sharing habits, there remains the sadness of not having reached "home," of not being able to share their nakedness on common ground, on which you can look and be looked at without fear of being derided or blocked.

Anna and Enrico are an elderly couple who have been together for 40 years. They are proud of what they have achieved in their family life—proud of their offspring and of the financial and relational solidity they have succeeded in creating. They are professionally very capable and independent, and this has on the one hand reinforced the proud solitude that has accompanied their attempts to contact each other, while on the other it has permitted them to "live on something else" to cover the pain of the wounds of intimacy with the gratifications of their working life. The limitation of social life that follows retirement has increased their incomprehensions—their life as a couple has become unbearable. As a result, they have turned to therapy:

Anna: I can't stand him reprimanding me in front of outsiders when I do something he doesn't like. I feel profoundly humiliated. I don't believe I deserve this treatment after a lifetime of sacrifices, both for our family and for him.

Enrico: The "sacrifices"—as you call them—were also made for your own benefit, don't think you're the only victim of this state of affairs. When I lose my cool, even in front of other people, I'm sorry, but it happens because you act as if I don't exist. You don't look at me; you make the decisions, maybe the right ones, but you visibly cut me out. And what am I for you? I've always loved you, I've even forgiven you and put up with times that I felt you were far off, and after all these years I don't deserve this treatment. It's very humiliating for me that you act in front of other people as if I don't exist.

Therapist: You both seem to have acquired a remarkable competence about the other's experiences over the years of your marriage. You each know what hurts the other and you each know how to make the other feel noticed and recognized in the sacrifices made. You also seem to know very well that the sense of humiliation linked to the other's reaction can be overcome—you have enough independence and personal security to forgive the other and not make them pay with an endless spiral of vindictiveness. You're capable of going beyond what you'd like in an ideal partner, of seeing what's in front of you and appreciating what the other has been doing for you for years. It seems that at these moments, when you feel the other's old wound, you keep on like a broken record with the same old patterns of defense against wounds, although you know they don't work. What's stopping you drawing closer together, with the tenderness you feel for each other after so many years of shared life? What happens when the other does something you don't like? You know you can forgive. Can you look at something else in him or her?

Anna: Right. At those times I know that the wound I feel isn't everything, yet it makes me angry that in all these years he hasn't learned to know me, to love me as I'd like. My feeling is that giving up what I'd like to get from him is like a leap in the dark, and it scares me. So I end up doing what I always do. It would be too risky for me to not get angry and to smile.

Enrico: What I could do at these times that would be different is smile and give her a kiss. I've occasionally done it, because I was asked to here, in therapy. It's like a magic gesture that puts everything right. But is it really so simple? And all those wounds, and frustrations, and disappointments that have gone hand in hand with our relationship—would they be solved with a smile and a kiss? It's too easy! Not to think about the wounds would be like sweeping away from the space between us all the memories of the things that I'd so much have loved to have from you and that I haven't had. I feel that smile would be like a leap in the darkness with you, like taking your hand and going towards life or death, it's not much different—towards whatever lies in store for us.

This sequence shows very clearly that for this couple quarrelling represents the best known way to overcome the anxiety of the relational void—"If I sweep away everything between us that reminds me of my wounds, of the ideal companion I was looking for in you, of the ideal person I nourished hopes of reaching as I had never done, I'll be face to face with YOU, a stranger. I'll please you, just you, not the person I imagined you had to be." It may seem odd, but many "old" couples find closeness unbearable precisely because of this anguish of the "naked" relationship.

What does a therapist do who believes in the value of spontaneity in couple systems?

> Rather than seeing creativity as a trait, property,
> or product of exclusively intrapsychic processes,
> [in Gestalt therapy] it is, instead, conceptualized
> as an aspect of relationship, existing between the
> self and the environment.
>
> Thus, the focus of creativity is shifted from
> something that resides in the interior of the
> person, to the dynamic of the individual in
> relation to the environment. Creativity then
> becomes a process that happens outside one's skin,
> "where the self meets the other."
>
> (Melnick & Nevis, 2003, p. 229)

The Gestalt therapist has a special approach to couple work—s/he believes that the aim of therapy is not the sacrifice of some individual wishes in favor of the rules of social living in the family, but rather the recovery of that *spontaneous creativity* which is the center of every meaningful relationship. The aim of Gestalt couple therapy is not to stop the partners from quarreling, but to facilitate their being capable of enjoying themselves and feeling alive, harmonious and creative at the contact boundary of their relationship. This may imply moments of conflict, passing through the pain of wounds caused by the other's behaviour. It may mean going through the humiliation of not feeling accepted by the other, but it certainly presupposes the aim of realizing intimacy with the other, the courage to express oneself to the other, not to sedate conflicts prematurely (Perls, 1942/1969).

The frame of reference of the Gestalt therapist is of a high standard. S/he is called to uphold an art, an innate capability, hard to explain in words, to be fully in the experience of contact, rather than transmit contents.

All the Gestalt therapists who have worked, and written about their work, with couples (for example: Lee, 1994, 1996, 2004; Lynch-Zinker, 1982; Lynch-Lynch, 2000; Lynch-Lynch, 2003; Melnick-Nevis,1987a; 1987b; 2003; Wheeler-Backman, 1994; Zinker, 1994; Zinker-Cardoso Zinker, 2001, and others), including Robert Lee in this book, beyond the specific details of their model, agree on a basic procedure which makes it possible to uphold this art in couples. The *first step* is to direct attention to what the couple already does well. In the very moment of discouragement when the couple asks for help, they have already spontaneously done something to function well. Drawing their attention to this is a great support which predisposes the partners to listen to the positive intentionalities of the other, beyond the perceived fears regarding her/his lack of acceptance. Joseph Zinker and Sandra Cardoso Zinker (2001) give an interesting and live example of what such a therapeutic intervention can be. During the process of the dialogue between the couple and between the therapists, which is worthwhile to read as a whole, Joseph at a certain moment (after a consultation with Sandra) says to the couple (who are strongly quarreling with each other): "You are a couple with a lot of energy.... You are fast using your language. You answer very fast each demand or statement that one or the other is making. You are doing very well in keeping your energy high. Being with you takes my breath away! Talk to each other about your impressions." And the couple replies: "It is strange to hear that to fight is good. It is true, we talk a lot" (p. 19). The authors explain: "Our emphasis is on their creative power as partners, an aesthetic entity as a system. We want to interest them.... in where they succeed and how they fail to reach each other.... We support the beauty and goodness of the couple; we support the process of their struggle, their pain" (p. 14).

Once this important change of atmosphere and perspective has been achieved ("I'm not here to accuse you or to be right, but to get to know you better") a *second stage* is that of bringing out what the partners would like to change about the other at the behavioral level. This implies training the partners in a *propositive* language—for example, "I would have liked you to ask me how I felt when you went away," or: "I don't mind you working with such satisfaction, even though this means that we can't be together as much as I'd like. I'm proud of you and of your job. I'd like you to ask me how I am from time to time, because that would make me feel that you're interested in me." This communicative strategy is important because it allows partners to harmonize with the other's intentionality of contact—the other's "complaint," which was formerly experienced as an accusation, is now understood as a wish for contact, for being accepted and considered capable of accepting the other.

When partners learn this communicative strategy and

choose it in awareness of the positive effects it creates in their ability to (re)cognize each other (in the etymological sense) beyond their fears, a *third step* is to focus on one's own and the other's intentionality of contact, so as to relate to each other against a background of reciprocity, rather than one of individual closures. *The other is not beside us to heal our old wounds, but to create a new relationship.*

This perspective of acceptance of novelty allows us to forgo healing our old wounds and this, paradoxically, allows us to see them differently. First we must accept that the other is not the ideal we created as the other side of the coin of our old wounds. The partners will thus be able to perceive each other for what each actually does for the relationship and for the other, radically modifying the former perception of the other as unaccepting, uninterested, as well as the perception of oneself as forced to become extraneous, forced to be unable to experience the yearned-for belonging. This is a revolutionary perceptive change.

To conclude

The blind enthusiasm to continue to risk despite our fears perhaps belongs more to the falling-in-love phase, regardless of how long that lasts in a couple. But getting through a crisis, looking the devil in the face—that devil which is metaphorically in the other—is the tribulation which is necessary if the experience of the couple is to represent a course of profound growth for the partners, a change of perception both of one's painful personal relational history and of the experience of the partner.

References

Beebe, B., & Lachmann, F. M. (2002). *Infant Research and Adult Treatment: Co-constructing Interactions.* New York: The Analytic Press.

Bloom, D. J. (2003). "Tiger! Tiger! Burning bright"—Aesthetic values as clinical values in Gestalt Therapy. In M. Spagnuolo Lobb & N. Amendt-Lyon (Eds.), *Creative License: The Art of Gestalt Therapy* (pp. 63-77). Vienna and New York: Springer.

Bloom. D. J. (2005), Laura Perls: The aesthetic of commitment, opening speech at the Conference "An der grenze," Laura Perls zum 100 geburtstag, München, Germany, delivered on June 3rd 2005 (unpublished)

Kitzler, R. (2003), Creativity as Gestalt Therapy. In M. Spagnuolo Lobb & N. Amendt-Lyon (Eds.), *Creative License: The Art of Gestalt Therapy* (pp. 101-111), Vienna and New York: Springer,.

Lee, R. G. (1994). Couples' shame: The unaddressed issue. In G. Wheeler & S. Backman (Eds.), *On Intimate Ground: A Gestalt Approach to Working with Couples* (pp. 262-290). San Francisco: Jossey-Bass.

Lee, R. G. (1996). The waif and Mr. Hyde: One couple's struggle with shame. In R. Lee & G. Wheeler (Eds.), *The Voice of Shame: Silence and Connection in Psychotherapy* (pp. 177-201). San Francisco: Jossey-Bass.

Lee, R. G. (2004). Working with couples: Application of Gestalt's values of connection. In R. G. Lee (Ed.), *The Values of Connection: A Relational Approach to Ethics* (pp. 159-177). Hillsdale, NJ: The Analytic Press/GestaltPress.

Lynch, B., & Zinker, J. (1982), Couples : How they develop and change. *Gestalt Newsletter*, GIC, 2: 1-4

Lynch, B., & Lynch, J. E. (2000). *Principles and Practices of Structural Family Therapy.* Highland, NY: The Gestalt Journal Press.

Lynch, B., & Lynch, E. (2003), Creativity in family therapy. In M. Spagnuolo Lobb & N. Amendt-Lyon (Eds.), *Creative License: The Art of Gestalt Therapy* (pp. 239-247). Vienna and New York: Springer.

Melnick, J., & March Nevis, S. (1987a). Power, choice and surprise. *Gestalt Journal*, 9:43-51.

Melnick, J., & March Nevis, S. (1987b). Gestalt family therapy. *British Gestalt Journal, 1*, 47-54

Melnick, J., & March Nevis, S. (2003), Creativity in long-term intimate relationships. M. Spagnuolo Lobb & N. Amendt-Lyon (Eds.), *Creative License: The Art of Gestalt Therapy* (pp. 227-238). Vienna and New York: Springer.

Perls, F. (1942/1969). *Introduction to Ego, Hunger and Agression: a Revision of Freud's Theory and Method*. London: N.Y, Random House.

Perls, F. S., Hefferline, R., & Goodman, P. (1951/1994). *Gestalt therapy. Excitement and Growth in the Human Personality*. Highland, New York: The Gestalt Journal Press,.

Searles, H. F. (1960). *The Non-Human Environment*. New York: International Universities Press.

Spagnuolo Lobb, M. (2001), The theory of self in Gestalt Therapy: A restatement of some aspects. *Gestalt Review*, 5(4):276-288.

Spagnuolo Lobb, M. (2003). Therapeutic meeting as improvisational co-creation. In M. Spagnuolo Lobb & N. Amendt-Lyon (Eds.). *Creative License: The Art of Gestalt Therapy* (pp. 37-49). Vienna and New York: Springer.

Spagnuolo Lobb, M. (2004). L'awareness dans la pratique post-moderne de la gestalt-therapie. *Gestalt, Societé Français de Gestalt* ed. XV(27):41-58. (transl. into Spanish: La consciencia inmediata en la pràctica post-moderna de la Terapia Gestalt. *Revista de Terapia Gestalt, Asociaciòn Española de Terapia gestalt*, No. 25, 2005, pp. 24-33).

Spagnuolo Lobb, M. (2005a). Classical Gestalt Therapy theory. In A. L. Woldt & S. M. Toman (Eds.), *Gestalt Therapy. History, Theory, and Practice* (pp. 21-39). Thousand Oaks, CA: Sage Publications, California.

Spagnuolo Lobb, M. (Ed.). (2005b). *Gestalt-thérapie Avec des Patients Sévèrement Perturbés*. Bordeaux: L'Exprimerie

Stern, D. N. (2004). *The Present Moment in Psychotherapy and Everyday Life*. New York: Norton.

Stern, D., Bruschweiler-Stern, N., Harrison, A., Lyons-Ruth, K., Morgan, A., Nahum, J., Sander, L., & Tronick, E. (1998a). The process of therapeutic change involving implicit knowledge: Some implications of developmental observations for adult psychotherapy. *Infant Mental Health J.*, 3: 300-308

Stern, D., Bruschweiler-Stern, N., Harrison, A., Lyons-Ruth, K., Morgan, A., Nahum, J., Sander, L., & Tronick, E. (1998b). Non-interpretive mechanisms in psychoanalytic therapy. The "something more" than interpretation. *Int J. Psycho-Anal.*, 79: 903-921

Stern, D., Bruschweiler-Stern, N., Harrison, A., Lyons-Ruth, K., Morgan, A., Nahum, J., Sander, L., & Tronick, E. (2000). Lo sviluppo come metafora della relazione. *Quaderni di Gestalt*, XVI(30/31):6-21.

Stern, D., Bruschweiler-Stern, N., Harrison, A., Lyons-Ruth, K., Morgan, A., Nahum, J., Sander, L., & Tronick, E. (2003). On the Other Side of the Moon. The Import of Implicit Knowledge for Gestalt Therapy. In M. Spagnuolo Lobb & N. Amendt-Lyon (Eds.). *Creative License: The Art of Gestalt Therapy* (pp.21-35). Vienna and New York: Springer.

Wheeler, G., & Backman, S. (1994). *On Intimate Ground: A Gestalt Approach to Working with Couples*, Hillsdale, NJ: The Analytic Press

Zinker, J. C. (1994). *In Search of Good Form: Gestalt Therapy with Couples and Family*, Cambridge, MA: GestaltPress

Zinker, J. C., & Cardoso Zinker, S. (2001). Process and silence. A phenomenology of couples therapy. *Gestalt Review*, 5 (1): 11-23.

Editor's Note:

Cultural and enviornmental influences play a significant role in couple partners' ability to relate to one another. Here Marina Ayo Balandrazo and Enrique Mercadillo Madero give us a compelling account of how couples in Mexico are caught between two formidable, outside forces—one emanating from traditional beliefs and values with strong intergenerational family ties and the other stemming from global development in Mexico that brings the promise of economic, professional, and social development with an individual focus.

In the process, Ayo and Mercadillo share with us the comprehensively sensitive, supportive, creative, and well articulated program they have developed to meet, understand and assist couples in finding their own path. We watch as Ayo deftly applies this attitude of acceptance and respect in working with a struggling couple.

7

•••••••••••••

Work with Couples in Mexico from a Gestalt Approach

Marina Ayo Balandrazo & Enrique Mercadillo Madero

W e humans are relational beings. Our readiness and need for relationship is inscribed in our genes. Our babies are born so unprepared and require long periods of parental care. To address this we have fashioned families and other social relationships that have helped us survive living on a planet filled with innumerable dangers. Thus, it is our nature and need in our daily lives to establish relationships with others, especially with those people who are significant within our affective universe.

At the same time, the relational patterns of interaction in our families are complex entities that are affected by a number of variables such as history, culture, and the nature of resources in the larger environment. As a culture accumulates sufficient history in dealing with a relatively static mix of environmental realities it develops strong family traditions that are meant to protect and to guide family life. These traditions, which regulate what attitudes and behaviors are permissible within the family, are honed and passed down from generation to generation, coming to reside in and be administered from the affective universe of each generation's parents. However, when newer alternatives become available in the larger environment, these traditions can be experienced as inflexible, hindering other ways of being in the world, by members of the younger generation, particularly by those entering adulthood.

During the last 20 years, Mexican, urban society couples have been immersed in a rapid processes of change, involving an extreme clash of values, beliefs and models for living. This process has brought members of this society considerable internal and relational tension. On one hand, the values of the traditional family prevail. Couples look to continue a close relationship with the extended family, following tradition and sustaining unity. This is supported and maintained by a hierarchical authoritarian system and by values more intimately tied to the religious model of Catholicism.

On the other hand, people are now being immersed, from a very young age, in the individualistic and global development paradigm, which promotes professional and economic success, individuality, more time for social rather than family relationships, and distribution of authority and labor between its members.

Couples in Mexico are caught in the middle, trying to achieve a balance between these two forces: On the one hand, the pressure to form a stable couple that sustains and nurtures the family and that adheres to traditional beliefs and values. On the other hand the demand of economic, professional and social development to be individualistic (as a couple as well as individuals). This is a battle between belonging and dependency in the family system and an independence that promises free choice of a path for its own sake.

It is very difficult for Mexican couples to achieve a balance between these opposing, equally powerful forces. We are immersed in a barrage of contradictory messages.

The level of information available and the immense exposure to fantasy oriented cultural models promoted by mass media greatly influence ideas and conceptions of what nowadays constitutes normal couple development and meaningful intimate interactions. Measuring themselves against such outside fantasy models can impair couple member's capacity to understand their relationship, leaving them open to feelings of shame and inadequacy. This lowers their sense of belonging in two major ways—by decreasing their sense of propriety towards the traditional family model and by increasing their feeling of being unable to fit into a changing, demanding and viable society.

Gestalt and Couples in Mexico

Students and practitioners of Gestalt in Mexico have been influenced in their training and development, in thought, philosophy, and therapeutic technique, by a variety of sources with diverse origins—from South America, with its cradle primarily in Argentina, to the beginnings of the experiential movement of Gestalt in California and finally to the Gestalt that has been developed within the movement known as "Human Development." It is the latter, with its praxis and theory which contemplates the principles and foundations of the development of the human potential, which has had the largest influence on us and to which we refer in this chapter.[1]

The socio cultural characteristics of Mexican urban society are predominantly influenced by a sense of confluent belonging that is perceived as necessary for the survival of the family as a whole. In this sense, the attitudes that support the maintenance and preservation of the family system, including those that impede development of "Self" functions, are perceived as good and necessary for the benefit of family health.

Experience in this type of Mexican family promotes confluence through limiting individuality and demeaning

---

[1] During the 70's several disciples of Perls began to teach in Mexico. Claudio Naranjo is one of the most recognized, and at the present time he still comes to the Yollocally center in Mexico and continues with his SAT Program. Jorge Espinoza, another disciple began to teach Gestalt in Guadalajara. He has had a strong influence in the humanistic movement as has Jerry Greenwald, who conducted several workshops in Mexico in the early 80's.

Hector Salama's work has been at the center of the Gestalt influence from Argentina. It's also important to mention the editorial work of Cuatro Vientos in Chile, which has had an enormous impact on Gestalt in Mexico.

Myriam Muñoz Polit is one of the most important influences in the Humanistic Gestalt Approach in Mexico. In 1985 she founded the Humanistic Gestalt Institute, and in the period since she has been a very strong pillar in the Gestalt movement in Mexico. The Humanistic Gestalt movement integrates the basics of the Centered Person Approach from Carl Rogers to the therapeutic work with traditional Gestalt.

differences, self-support and the development of non-family relationship networks. At the same time, family dependency is fostered through such family beliefs and interactional forms as gender differentiation. The man is permitted to engage in attitudes and behaviors that are denied to the woman and vice versa, creating and maintaining distance, envy and distrust between men and women.

Securing a continuance of traditional family affective unity is sought beyond all else, even at the cost of the development and growth of any family member. It is common in Mexico to meet single people in their thirties who still live with their parents, since it reflects poorly on parents if a child leaves home if the child is yet to be married or if such a move is not required by education or professional development.

The price of this confluence with traditional family beliefs, around permissible thought and affective experience, is a blunting of the development of "Self" functions and of the capacity to self-sustain, yearnings for which are exiled from consciousness. In the process, the person (generally during childhood) abdicates his/her own sense of experience and competencies because of his/her need to "fit" within the family, thus completing and maintaining the self-sustaining cycle of dependency.

Without support for children to develop as individuals within the family context as they grow, they do not acquire the foundation they need later to establish a healthful interdependence through the establishment of mutually supportive social networks. In Mexico, these networks are replaced in adult life by the family structure. There are situations and experiences that can never leave this closed nucleus. Anyone sharing family material, which is always deemed as sacredly secret, with "outsiders" will be violently rejected by the rest of the family system.

Double standards, conveyed through mixed verbal and non-verbal communication, are common—for example, it is said that having sexual relationships before marriage is wrong, but when a father finds out that his son has had his first sexual experience, regardless of relational context, he feels proud. For the woman it is the opposite, she can be expelled from the family system even if it is revealed that she has had sexual relations with her betrothed before getting married.

In these systems, boundaries between family members are extremely permeable or non-existent, which not only promotes personal shame but also drives an internal family shame that complicates even more member's individual development. Instead of developing and relying on a system of relationship networks that support growth, what forms is emotional isolation maintained through the fear of personal and family secrets being exposed. As a result boundaries are rigidly closed to family-field contact and forced open in person-family relationships.

This relationship scheme makes it difficult to move towards the development of responsible self-sustainment and promotes toxic dependency. Before the eighties, the situation was even more severe. In general, couple's relational experience was extremely unsatisfactory, with great affective distance since each partner maintained a good part of his/her emotional life in secret and replaced it with fulfilling traditionally defined rolls or by engaging in diverse forms of unfaithfulness.

Gender roll differentiation abounds in traditional families, promoting mutual dependency, distance and distrust. It is common to see women depending economically and socially on their father, then later depending on their husband and finally on their own children. At the same time it is off-limits for men to engage in domestic chores of caring and affective relationship with their children, activities for them that bring ridicule and humiliation.

In this dependent relationship what blooms is the formation of traditionally defined rolls since, due to couple members' attachment to rigid and introjected values, this is seen as what supports and "guarantees" the survival of the couple. Unfortunately, this limits the co-creative capacity of the couple to make their own path.

Since the eighties and in present times, through globalization and the abundant supply of information, Mexican urban society has begun to incorporate new values and patterns, fostering new desires and yearnings, which differ radically from the ones promoted in the traditional family. Not unsurprisingly, this societal change brings with it the development of a double system of shame—both shame derived from the family scheme and shame stemming from a sense of inadequacy in meeting the new social demands.

Traditionally, the cycle of toxic dependency is set to continue in the couple from their earliest beginnings since it is expected that couple members arrive after having exiled a significant part of their Self from consciousness and with a series of strongly assimilated family introjects. In this broth of culture, dependency is promoted once again since couple members, as their childhood development has spurned individuality, have been programmed to pass from one scheme of parental dependency, based on shame, to a new scheme with their partner, also threatening. Since depending on each other, in accordance with what couple members believe is expected of them, does not offer them the experience of responsible self-sustainment, this new relationship will generate resentments and secrets that will reconstitute the shame scheme once again.

Working Model

Our working model emanates from the above-mentioned principles. It includes a phenomenological approach, the value of the present, and a grounding of empathy and acceptance toward the creative mode in which this unique couple has found to survive and grow. We value flexibility, spontaneity, authentic dialogic encounter, and the use of experiment as the primary path to learn in the here and now.

UPAD (Unit of Psychotherapy, Consultancy and Development, A. C.), is a center of psychotherapy and training which has operated in three cities (Guadalajara, Monterrey and Irapuato) for more than 10 years. Over this period we have developed a model that is based on the attitudes of acceptance, presence and deep encounter, in which we respect and support the expression of feelings and meaning. We use a phenomenological approach in meeting couples, as that allows us to experience the relationship as the members of the couple perceive it in the moment that they are with us.

With the above as ground, and with the consideration that we deem each encounter to be unique, we describe below the general phases of our model.

Therapeutic model for working with couples in Mexico.

I   Establishment and maintenance of the therapeutic relationship.
   A   Couple arrival and creation of therapeutic climate.
   B   Voicing of reasons and fears related to coming to therapy.
   C   Perception of the state of the relationship by each couple member.
   D   Voicing of and support for the individual motivations for selection of the other as a partner.
   E   Preliminary agreements.
II Conflict handling.
   A   Listening to the other's experience.
   B   Working with introjections and polarities.
   C   Modeling listening and empathy.
   D   Acquisition and development of nurturant intimacy skills.
   E   Expression of movements of mutual influence.
III Development of abilities and skills for creative intimacy.
   A   Attention and listening to feelings and meanings.
   B   Expression of esteem and nurturing differences.
   C   Expression of mutual influence.

Establishment and maintenance of the therapeutic relationship in a context of acceptance and psychological security

It is common that couples arrive in therapy and begin the initial session with a sense of distrust and shyness, since in Mexico therapeutic support is still commonly seen as an "outsider's solution," fit only for those who are "crazy" or "sick." A frequently held value is that the couple must solve its conflicts and difficulties by itself or with support from relatives or priests (the population is predominantly catholic).

By "establishment of the relationship" we mean creating a welcoming, warm atmosphere through informal talk at the beginning of each session, which allows the therapist to be included in the couple system and facilitates the formation of a relationship with each couple member. This initial time of casual interaction with the couple, offers a non-threatening setting for the couple in which we are able to observe the couple's style of engagement and retreat. Also, it allows us to listen to tones, pacing, glances, postures and gestures, all of which provides valuable information about and facilitates our meeting the unique being of this couple in this given moment.

It is important to note that this approach (first step), is used to start every session. This also allows the couple to make some space from the energy they bring with them on arrival (traffic, timing problems and other elements of pressure) before entering the therapeutic atmosphere. We have found that little by little, couple members learn from this experience and begin, in a natural way "to close" and to make assimilation spaces between one gestalt and another in their daily lives.

Our next focus in the initial session is to request that each couple member explain their motivation in coming to see us, as well as what they expect from this process. In this endeavor, we are interested in and we devote considerable empathic and respectful attention to hearing not only the stated reasons but even more importantly the underlying intentions (yearnings) of both couple members. As we listen, we empathically receive and underline couple member's feelings and meanings, and the impact that hearing this is having on the other.

In this sense, neuro-scientific discoveries suggest that change and learning have to do with emotion and meaning.[2] This

---

[2] For example, Ramachandran (2006) describes the astonishing findings on mirror neurons in research on monkeys:

... any given mirror neuron will also fire when the monkey in question observes another monkey (or even the experimenter) performing the same action, e.g. tasting a peanut! With knowledge of these neurons, you have the basis for understanding a host of very enigmatic aspects of the human mind: "mind reading" empathy, imitation learning, and even the evolution of language. Anytime you watch someone else doing something (or even starting to do something), the corresponding mirror neuron might fire in your brain, thereby allowing you to "read" and understand another's intentions, and thus to develop a sophisticated "theory of other minds." (I suggest, also, that a loss of these mirror neurons may explain autism—a cruel disease that afflicts children. Without these neurons the child can no longer understand or empathize with other people emotionally and therefore completely withdraws from the world socially.) (p. 2) provides theoretical support for our work. Along the same line, many educational fields stress that learning is most powerful where there is an emotional component, not just cognitive material. Since in our society the cognitive approach is more developed, we emphasize the recognition, assimilation and communication of both emotion and meaning (emotion plus thought), that takes us directly to intimacy and closeness.

Also this allows us to clarify the limits of therapy in the course of the dialogue with the couple. We have found that in Mexican society, saying the rules and limits without a dialogic context is perceived as aggressive, distant, non-caring and cold, which produces an effect of a "totally inadequate medical frame" for our model. Thus, we chose to use the couple's own speech to introduce, in a more colloquial manner, the rules and limits that can be expected from the therapeutic encounter, clarifying at the same time any fears and unrealistic ideas about the process.

Finally, in this first session we facilitate the establishment of a provisional agreement around the points of tension that each member of the couple perceives in the relationship and how each couple member contributes to the maintenance of such tension. This tends to generate a sense of power and hope within couple members by promoting the recognition that the situation is not only something that is outside their control, but also, through developing a deeper awareness of themselves and each other, they also generate a capacity to respond (capacity to choose), which is the path to freedom.

To close the initial session we facilitate a deeper heart-felt connection between couple members, which balances the air of conflict they have been experiencing. We ask them such things as: How did you fall in love with each other? What do you appreciate about being a couple? In what way does your couple nourish or satisfy you? We caringly, and emphatically encourage their answering, which generally leads to nostalgic feelings, sweetness, and hope.

To illustrate the above, consider the example of Mara and Andrés, a couple in their 30´s that comes to therapy because the recent death of Andrés father has brought overwhelming tension to their relationship. They have two small children, 6 years and 2 months old respectively. They have been together for ten years, the last four of which they have been married.

Both come from traditional but nevertheless quite different families. Whereas Mara perceives her family as affectionate and a little "metiche,"[3] Andrés perceives his as closed, authoritarian and violent. Mara presents with an adolescent quality. The first thing that catches one's attention is her full, tender and bright eyes. Andrés, on the other hand, presents with great sadness, which he tries to disguise by making jokes.

After casual talk about the traffic and the difficulties to find parking, Marina starts the session:

Marina: What brings you here?
Andrés: My father passed away some months ago (his
        eyes fill with tears and Mara takes his hand)

---

[3] Mexican term that indicates that someone has the capacity to intrude on other people's business.

and I have not been able to recover. He was a great man and he taught us to be strong and brave, but I miss him so much and am not sure if I can continue without him. He taught us many values: truth, honesty... He taught us to work and to be good people.

Mara: (interrupting) Speak about your sisters.

Andrés: (turns in his seat) I am going to... Soon after we buried him, a woman came to see me, saying to me that she was my father's daughter and that she had another sister. She brought birth certificates, photographs and other things as proof that my father had another family in secret. Of course neither my brothers nor I have told my mother because of the suffering it would mean for her.

Marina: It must have been a very painful surprise.

Andrés: In the beginning I could not believe it, but talking to them, I found out that other people, near to my father, also knew.

Mara: Since the death of his father, Andrés is angrier with the children, more intransigent. He wants us to be with his family each weekend. And he wants me to take the children to his mother almost every day. His family is very "macho" and he wants me to act like the women in his family—I am not supposed to speak my opinions, nor say anything when they tell jokes about women and "mandilones" (men that are submissive to women).

Andrés: What I want is that you do not cause trouble for us. You know how my brothers are.

Mara: (raising her voice) But, why must I shut up? I don't like this. I don't want you to be like them.

Andrés: You know that I am not like that. But it is my family.

Marina: I can imagine how difficult it must be for you to find yourselves in this situation and to deal with all the feelings which you have to face as a couple—with each other as well as with regard to your parents and to members of your larger family.

Andrés: I know I am depressed and that I have not been able to overcome the loss of my father. But I am better than the others. At least I am not getting drunk every weekend like them.

By this time I had a clear sense that staying with punishments and recriminations would only recycle us in an endless battle, and I decided to use a metaphor to move the discussion to a different plane.

Marina: When I listen to the two of you, I have the feeling that you are surrounded by a tornado, and I see you wanting to grab on to something so as to not be swept away by the tornado.

But as all is a blur in tornados, your efforts have no results... I ask myself if it is possible for you to find something that will keep you safe within the tornado?

Mara: (turning to Andrés) Aha!.. If we do what you say, everything we have fought to get will be lost and we will have a family like the ones of your brothers... Is that what you want?

Andrés: You know that I don't... (turning to Marina) Explain to me about the tornado. How do we get there?... I do feel lost and alone, fighting against my brothers who make fun that Mara commands me, and fighting against Mara so that she doesn't shame me in their eyes.

Marina: How could you survive in the tornado?

Mara: I would take hold of Andrés with all my might, and he would take hold of a tree or a huge rock that would hopefully protect us until the tornado has passed.

Andrés: For me?... If I am in a tornado, I would not know what to leave or what to save!

Mara: We don't have to leave anything. We just need to survive while the tornado passes... I take hold of you and you of a strong tree, we would not get lost. (crying)

Andrés: (embracing her)... We are going to get through this... don't cry... Before, that tree was my father... but he fell. He was not so big.

(with a broken voice)... Embraced we will wait for the tornado to pass.

Marina: How do you feel?

Andrés: I feel strong hugging Mara...

Mara: (straightening her self and remaining embraced). Good!... (smiles)...

Marina: What have you learned from this experience?

Andrés: That by embracing, we can weather the tornado and that I was grabbing a tree that was not so safe. I need to find another one.

Mara: Same as him. I feel very alone when I see him lost.

Marina: Do you have an idea of what tree might shelter you?

Mara: That is the reason for coming here, to find that.

Andrés: (in silence, nods his head affirmatively)

Marina: I understand that you are in search of a refuge for difficult times that is safer than your father, Andrés.

Andrés: Yes, that tree was not so big...

Marina: Seeing you embrace each other and the connection that exists between you, takes me to what I would like to ask you next. Do you remember what led you to want to marry each other... that is to say, what you saw, that made you like the other so much it made you want to share your life with the other?

Mara: Andrés was a Don Juan, but with me he always behaved like a gentleman. He protected me from others. He was very happy and sociable. He was always good with my friends; he was very affectionate, a very hard worker and very formal...

Andrés: (stirring himself in the chair). I was always a bit of a vagabond, but not bad. I remember that when I was fourteen, I secretly took my father's car to pickup Mara and take her to the cinema. When I returned home, he gave me a beating, but it was worth the trouble. Soon my brother, Rogelio, lent me his car to take Mara to parties in exchange for my being his servant the rest of the week. That didn't last long though; he just stopped lending it to me. I then used my father's car, until he lent me money to buy one... (turning to Mara) You remember?

Mara: I remember you got angry a lot... Rogelio always was very abusive.

Marina: Andrés, what did you like about Mara that made you want to marry her?

Andrés: Mara has always been a happy woman, very affectionate and warm. A hard worker... Until we had the baby, we traveled a lot because she worked in a travel agency. It was a very happy time.

Marina: How do you feel?

Mara: Good. (directing a smile to Andrés)

Andrés: Happy, I believe that we can live with the tornado...

Marina: Mara, I remember you saying that you had hope that you would find refuge from the tornado here in therapy...

Mara: I believe that here we can do what we did today and feel again that we are a family, and that Andrés can address what happens to him... Don't you think? (looking at Andres)

Andrés: I need to speak about my father and my family without you criticizing them. It is very important to me that you understand—that you take care of me and love me.

Marina: I hear that you both need to support the other. I ask myself if you realize how each one of you contributes to the other feeling alone.

Andrés: I have been immersed in my pain and in very bad humor, and I have taken it out on Mara and the children. But I need Mara to understand and be patient with me.

Mara: I loose patience when you ask too much of me when I must also take care of the children. I understand you, but there is only so much that I can give, and I loose patience.

Marina: What would you like to ask from Andrés?

Mara: That he has breakfast after I take Andrecito to
school. That way I would be able to take care
of both of them.

Marina: Andrés, is there someway that you can
support this need of Mara?

Andrés: There is no problem, I can have some coffee
while I wait and have breakfast later. But leave
the soap in the bath before going out...
(laughing)

Mara: (also laughing) I only forgot once... Maybe we
can be calm before you leave...

Marina: Shall we make an appointment for next week,
at which time we can review how this
adjustment has worked out?

Andrés: Yes, let's see if I am not fatter with a daily
breakfast.

Mara: As if you do not eat your sandwiches at work.

Andrés: Of ham and cream of Santa Tere...

Marina: Well, I will have the scale ready when you
come in.

Conflict handling

Couples usually encounter their greatest difficulty around
negotiating their differences. In Mexico this process becomes
even more difficult, as couple members' vision is often blurred by
their fears and lessons from the past (introjects and unfinished
businesses) that lead them to respond with rigid and

authoritarian patterns that generally deepen the abyss, leaving them alone and hopeless.

It has been a welcome surprise for us to read Lee and Wheeler's (e.g., 1996) writings on shame in general and Lee's description of shame in a couple system (Lee, 1994, 1996, 2004, and the beginning chapters of this book) in particular. These conceptualizations fit with our experiences of therapeutic work. The recognition that the secret language of shame is the result of a loss of belonging, that permeates the relationship and appears like a curtain dropped on unmanageable conflicts, allows us to go deeper in the experience of the couple and to obtain a fuller communication and understanding, generating intimacy and respectful belonging.

It is common, in couples that we see, that fears of humiliation and abandonment become reactivated in conflicts, without couple members awareness—e.g., feelings of shame disguised with coldness, authoritarianism, and violence, or with self-denial, manipulation and dependency.

So, as we mentioned in the beginning of the article, couples in Mexico face a double tension—on the one side, to maintain the traditions of the extended family and on the other side, to be successful in a world heavily influenced by values of individual development and professional recognition.

Also as mentioned, a great disparity exists between gender roles in Mexico. Although this has started to be questioned and the distance between gender roles narrowed to some extent, the situation continues to be severe in many cases. It is very common that men feel pressured by women for protection and guidance. This pressure is at times expressed openly by women and at other times disguised through submission and self-denial, and other strategies women use for comfort and security in the face of the authoritarian atmosphere they have come to expect.

The male answer in general is to dissuade oneself of one's internal world and employ rigidity and authoritarianism in one's relationship. Often it seems that the husband is more father and/or son to his spouse than her companion, at the same time that the woman plays a double roll of mother and daughter to her husband. The traditional family in Mexico demands "stern, strong and formal" men, coexisting with "good, silent and sacrificing" women who give their life to the well-being and development of their husband and children.

As a consequence of these dynamics, any difference of opinions, ways to perceive the world or attempts to change the established rolls, by either couple member, leads to blame and threats of family destruction. Not only is the result difficult to handle by itself, it also leads to additional feelings of inadequacy and shame for both members.

We identify five elements that are important in conflict resolution between couple members:

Listening to the experience of the other implies not only the content, but even more importantly the feelings and meanings. The latter are often tied to obsolete and rigid experiences from the past and have served to signal and negotiate vulnerable and humiliating situations. However, they may have also impeded the development of mature and updated abilities.

Through phenomenological exploration, in which preconceived judgments are held to a minimum with the protection of the therapist, each member of the couple learns to express his/her experiences and to deepen their meaning. In the process, experiences from the past that are influencing couple member's present vision in the conflict are clarified.

In this stage, it is very important for the therapist to set the tone with an initial clear and direct statement of the intentions and goals of this stage as well as what is required by each member. In particular, the therapist must stress the value of and ask for an attitude of loving and respectful listening by all in response to either couple member speaking. (Polster & Polster, 1973)

We ask permission from both members of the couple to intervene specifically with one of them (as this is a boundary modification with which couples would not normally be familiar). At such times the other couple member listens and is peripheral momentarily. When this intervention finishes, invariably we invite the couple member that has been listening, to express his/her own experiences with this subject by speaking directly to his/her partner. This restores the couple system boundaries, while the therapist retires to his position of companion of both. (Zinker, 1998).

Andrés: Mara and I have lived like brothers for months now because she says that she fears getting pregnant again. (turning to Mara) Even your mother said that it was dangerous for you to have an operation, because if we later want to have children we would not be able to. I already said to you that I am going to have an operation as soon as I speak with my friend. He says he can help me with my concern about losing energy as a result of the operation.

Mara: You have been saying that for more than two weeks, and still you have not spoken with your friend. I am tired of it. If you don't have an operation, I will.

Andrés: It is not something I can do over the telephone. We need to see each other, to sit down and have time to talk. This is very important. I don't want to rush into something and later regret it... Also, if I have an operation, you will be sure that I am not going to have children "scattered" somewhere. (laughing)

Mara: Right!, Well that's your problem, not mine. What I don't want is to get pregnant again.

Andrés: And don't even think about talking about this with my family. I already said to you that if we do it, it is something between you and me. And also please tell that to your parents! It makes me mad to hear them talk about it casually, let alone that they know about it. It is a serious thing Mara, and you take it very lightly. I almost fell off my chair when your mother asked me in front of everyone if I had decided to have the operation. If your father had not spoken about his operation, I believe that I would have left the room.

Mara: What is wrong with you? It is normal for people to talk about such things with family. Don't think every family is like yours.

Andrés: Again, the same thing. I hate it when you compare your family and mine. Marina, we are stuck in the same place; the end result is always that her family is better than mine. I've had it!

Both turn toward me, and I feel their wanting me to intervene. It seems to me that underlying factors are impeding their ability to process the issue of birth control that they are trying to handle. Andrés appears to be in a one-down position; coming from a more conventional, secretive and impulsive family makes him more vulnerable. I sense that Mara tends to use Andrés' family's attributes to position herself as an oppressed victim. This combination hinders the support that they give each other and thus keeps them off-balance and keeps the conflict from being solved. Andrés has just asked for help with this underlying factor, and I decide to intervene initially with him.

Marina: I have the impression that there are two important issues for the two of you: the decision of how to avoid new pregnancies and how much discretion about that is important for each one of you. I would like, if you do not have any objections, to explore this first with you Andrés.

Andrés: Good.

Marina: Is this alright with you, Mara?

Mara: It's OK.

Marina: For this I need you Mara to just listen, with kindness, to Andrés' experience, monitoring what is happening to you in response to what he says, so that later you can comment about that.

Mara: It is OK...

Marina: (directly to Andrés). I see that the thought of speaking about birth control with your or Mara's family is very disturbing to you...

Andrés: Yes, it makes me mad that Mara is so outspoken and that she speaks about everything... If my family knows about it, their jokes will be relentless. I'll never get them off my back. Not only will my brothers make fun of me, it will give them more ammunition to make comments on how Mara controls me.

Marina: I imagine that you have been the brunt of their ridiculing jokes in the past.

Andrés: Yes, that is the way it is in my house. Once they take hold of you, they won't let go.

Marina: And how do you feel when this happens?

Andrés: Well how do you think? They all make fun of
me, and I have to shut up, because if I say any
thing, they will laugh more.

Marina: It must have been very hard to live like this as
a boy.

Andrés: Yes, with my father it was worse... I preferred
to be beaten than to have them make fun of
me. The physical blows don't hurt nearly as
much... It was horrible... For weeks at a time
I'd have to endure the same jokes over and
over, and I had to restrain myself (his face
reddens and his eyes look down). And then,
whenever I wanted something, the jokes would
start up again.

Marina: I get a picture of how you had to keep your
anger silent and how you felt humiliated and
trapped.

Andrés: Yes, it was horrible. I would go outside by
myself and throw stones because I was so
angry. But whenever I did, I would end up
crying, feeling ashamed because I was too
sensitive. I don't want to go through that
again; I still don't know how to defend myself.

Marina: It saddens me to imagine how angry, sad,
and alone you were as a boy... Andrés, if you
could go back now as an adult and see the
boy that you were, throwing stones and crying,
what would you do?

Andrés: (Silence.. and after a moment). I would stay with him, and ask him to tell me what happened... I would give him a hug and tell him that he is a good boy, that the other kids are fools by treating him like that... that they are abusive and that I am pleased he is not like them. And I would throw stones with him so that he doesn't have to keep that poison inside... (makes visual contact with me)

Marina: I hear that you are proud of being different from them...

Andrés: Yes, very proud. I do not make fun of anyone that cannot defend himself...

Marina: How do you feel now?

Andrés: Moved... well... I feel stronger and more complete...

Marina: Would you be willing to listen to what Mara has to say?

Andrés: Yes.

Marina: How do you feel about this Mara?

Mara: (Addressing Andrés). It makes me very sad and angry that they treated you like that... (crying and taking his hands) I can almost see you and I wish I could have been there with you... I also would have thrown rocks with you... I love you very much... I thank God that you are not like them.

Andrés: That is why I do not want you to tell them about this. I do not want them to make fun of this... but I also do not want us to have to hide from them. Right now I don't know what to do...

Mara: I think that you and I can talk about this and agree on what to do...

Working with polarities in the couple. As part of the couple's system, conflict between couple members frequently leads to experiencing the other as bad, wrong, and unreliable, and experiencing oneself as good, right and reliable, independently of the conflict content.

Also we have observed, through the years of being with couples, if the polarities are not assimilated, they tend to repeat, with only the roles changing, but not the game. That is to say, the couple member who initially played the oppressor role, through time plays the role of the one who is oppressed, likewise the pursuer plays the one who is pursued, and so on. In the therapeutic encounter it is important to have couple members recall what it was like to be in the other roll. This provides a source of empathy for the other's current position.

We consider the work of the therapeutic encounter, in this phase, to consist of providing, on one side the acquisition and assimilation of the disowned polarity, which has come to be thought of as solely residing in one's companion and not in oneself. On the other side, we facilitate couple partners developing the self-knowledge that allows them to detect when this is happening; so that they may avoid unnecessary suffering and deepen their intimacy.

We are reminded of Andrea, who for more than 10 years of marriage conducted her life and personal interests based on the principle of fulfilling the requirements of her husband, Salvador, and their 2 children. After a process of individual psychotherapy, she modified her style, leading her to openly express her necessities and desires. When they started couples therapy, somewhat later, it was Salvador who was having difficulty and was on the verge of giving up because regardless of how hard he tried to please his wife, it was not enough. On helping them reflect on how easy it is to move from oppressed to oppressor and vice versa, that both oppressed and oppressor are facets of the same coin, they could walk towards greater freedom and respect for one another.

Modeling listening and empathy on the part of the therapist, sometimes is done explicitly, and other times accomplished through a sort of learning "in situ" so that the couple learns, develops and integrates these abilities into its relationship.

For this we request that the couple talk about something together, with the therapist acting as an observer and intervening when necessary, or when one of the members requires it. Initially, couples are often uncomfortable with this process, and some resist this procedure. In those cases we explore the couple's concerns with them. Generally, couples may fear that they will be evaluated, criticized, or humiliated in some manner by the therapist or by the experience.

If after this exploration, which in many cases stems from lessons they have had to learn in the past, they continue to have objections, we ask them to imagine some other way in which they could develop these abilities. At the same time we provide additional structural support for the couple ranging from homework assignments, to exchanging notes and letters, to role plays in which the therapist takes the role of one of the members while that member becomes the therapist.

We have found that couples have very creative solutions to learning, which has also increased our confidence to open ourselves to their unique ideas.

Acquisition of nurturant intimacy skills. Lee (1994) found in his research that the couples with skills of reception and connection had low levels of ground shame and a high sense of emotional safety. Also there is a secret language of shame, as well as a language of intimacy and belonging.

During this stage, we pay attention to and underline what the couple does that implies belonging, such as glances, gestures, anecdotes, and special words that each couple uses to show affection and understanding. We devote time and attention to acknowledging when the couple risks moments of nurturance and intimacy, exploring what they did to facilitate that happening.

Jerry Greenwald (1975) points to the skills of conscience, communication and confrontation, as the antidotes of toxicity in relationships. From this base, we derive experiences in which the expression of differences as well as of necessities and yearnings, are listened to, and received and then responded to by the companion.

We pay attention to nonverbal signs that indicate not only possible experiences of shame (cold, empty, shrinkage, looking down/away, muscular tension, and the like) but which also indicate experiences of connection (mutual gazing or looking directly at each other, exhibiting an internal warmth, relaxation, deep breathing), to extend the tools which the couple has for communicating.

Expression of the movements of mutual influence. As the process of self-awareness and awareness of the internal world of one's companion advances, couple members can more clearly view the effects that their behavior and particularly their attitudes have on their partner.

Each couple has its zones of sensitivity, where attitudes of one companion "touch" shame nuclei that lead to exaggerated responses from the other. The respectful and loving awareness of these sensitivity zones allows couple members to express their vulnerability. Slowly as confidence increases, they can expose the areas in which they have a sense of confusion, inadequacy, and fear.

This road to vulnerability awareness generally strengthens the ties of the couple in a unique and special way, which generates a sense of belonging and acceptance, which in turn is the antidote for shame.

Development of abilities and skills for creative intimacy. During the process of therapy couple members accumulate experiences in which their conflictual differences are transformed, through expression and reception of their underlying yearnings and vulnerability, to a sense of connection and intimacy. In the process they develop a respect for each other and an ability to listen.

The couple relationship offers a unique opportunity for intersubjective interaction between equals in a safe, nurturant atmosphere. This privileged relationship allows us the chance to encounter newness, discover facets of ourselves, and build a joint awareness and understanding of life's mysteries, with another, in a manner and depth which is not possible in any other type of relationship.

Thus, the complexity and the risks inherent in a couple relationship are very much worth the trouble, for the individuals as well as for the success of the relationship.

Final Words

In Mexico we are living a double revolution. We believe that the challenge for couples is finding and mastering the path to intimacy instead of attempting to maintain confluence with traditional values. The price of the latter is sacrificing couple members' sense of experience, which leads to emotional isolation and a sense of emptiness.

References

Greenwald, J. (1973). *Be the Person You Were Meant to Be*. New York: Simon & Shuster.

Greenwald, J. (1975). *Creative Intimacy*. New York: Jove Books.

Lee, R. G. (1994). Couples' shame: The unaddressed issue. In G. Wheeler & S. Backman (Eds.), *On Intimate Ground: A Gestalt Approach to Working with Couples* (pp.262-290). San Francisco: Jossey-Bass.

Lee, R. G. (1996). The waif and Mr. Hyde. In R. G. Lee and G. Wheeler (Eds.), *The Voice of Shame: Silence and Connection in Psychotherapy* (pp. 177-201). San Francisco: Jossey-Bass.

Lee, R. G. (2004). Working with couples: Application of Gestalt's values of connection. In R. G. Lee (Ed.), *The Values of Connection: A Relational Approach to Ethics* (pp. 159-177). Hillsdale, NJ: GestaltPress/The Analytic Press.

Lee, R. G., & Wheeler, G. (Eds.). (1996). *The Voice of Shame: Silence and Connection in Psychotherapy.* San Francisco: Jossey-Bass.

Marcos, R. M., (1994) La pareja rota. Madrid, España: Espasa Calpe Editores .

Polster, I., & Polster, M. (1973). *Gestalt Therapy Integrated: Contours of Theory and Practice.* New York: Brunner/Mazel.

Ramachandran, V. S. (2006). Mirror Neurons and imitation learning as the driving force behind "the great leap forward" in human evolution. Edge.org http://www.edge.org/3rd_culture/ramachandran/ramachandran_p1.html

Wheeler, G., & Backman S. (Eds.) (1994). *On Intimate Ground: A Gestalt Approach to Working with Couples.* San Francisco: Jossey-Bass.

Wheeler, G. (2005). *Vergüenza y Soledad.* Santiago, Chile: Editorial cuatro vientos.

Zinker, J. (1998). *In Search of Good Form: Gestalt Therapy with Couples and Families.* Hillsdale, NJ: GestaltPress/The Analytic Press.

Editor's Note:

Ed and Barbara Lynch, senior clinicians, trainers, and writers in the field, have been working with couples and families, and training and supervising couple and family therapists for over 25 years. From their university setting in Connecticut, USA, they bring us their unique voice, schooled by their extensive experience, their diverse theoretical background, and their warm and generous presence.

Here they focus on the importance of appreciating family of origin contributions to the hidden taboos and knots that interfere with couple partner's ability to relate to one another. They provide us with a broader understanding of the components and complexity of intimacy and share with us a "projective" technique that they have long used in helping couples discover the relational patterns in their family of origin.

8

• • • • • • • • •

Understanding the
Complexity of Intimacy

Barbara J. & J. Edward Lynch

Intimacy is both an elusive and sought after factor in relationships. The foundation and the structure of the relationship reside in the capacity for intimacy, the struggle to attain it, and the intrinsic anxiety associated with having it and losing it. In thirty years of working with couples, it has become apparent that individuals choose partners with an unspoken agreement that the capacity for intimacy in the dyad and the manner in which intimacy is expressed is learned at an early age, out of awareness, and that the threshold for intimacy is established from families of origin.

Individuals "learn" a comfortability and/or an anxiety/shame associated with intimacy from interactions that take place in family of origin settings. These patterns are established in early childhood and remain operational in a subtle and powerful manner throughout the individual's life. Therapists working with clients on their issues with intimacy can spend many hours in efforts designed to uncover these patterns and to make inferences from the therapeutic relationship about the template of intimacy governing the client's relationships.

Starting with the premise that the client's self-discovery will neutralize resistance and be more enduring as a self-creation than an interpretation by the therapist, a reliable tool for encouraging self-discovery, in uncovering such patterns, is desirable and helpful. The authors have developed and used a "projective" technique with individuals and couples for more than twenty-five years with results that are resoundingly successful. Individuals are asked to represent their family of origin as they experienced it when they were either ten, eleven, or twelve years old. A series of four geometric figures, shown in Figure 1, are used as symbols to represent individual family members.

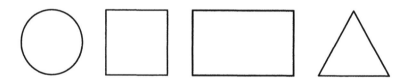

Figure 1: Symbols Used in Family Diagrams

In and of themselves these basic four shapes have no significance or interpretative value. Consistent with a systemic perspective, shapes are relevant only as they are related to, and are different from and/or similar to, another shape. In this regard, the factors of proximity and distance, identification, and restricted (or unrestricted) access to other figures, and relative size as an indication of perceived power are given consideration.

Using diagrams of intimate partners, allows the couple to recognize their areas of similarity and differences that have an impact on their inherent capacity for intimacy and their areas of potential difficulty. As an example, consider the family of origin diagrams of Betty and Jack, a couple who have been married 14 years and who have been experiencing increasing difficulty:

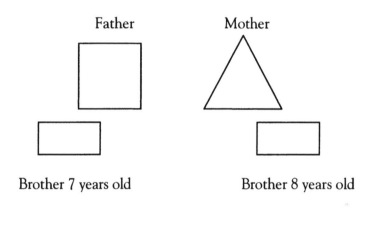

Father Mother

Brother 7 years old   Brother 8 years old

Betty age 10

Figure 2: Betty's Family Diagram

A consideration of the arrangement of symbols presented in Betty's drawing offers clues as to the dynamics that existed in

Betty's family of origin. In practice, it is the couple that uses their family diagrams as tools in their process of self discovery (see Notes on Using the Diagram Exercise). For the purpose of illustrating the nature and range of information that the couple can obtain from this exercise, a hypothetical set of symbol patterns that may be seen in Betty's family diagram is presented below:

1. Betty's symbol for herself is the symbol that is most distant from others in the diagram.

2. Betty's brothers are pictured closer to a parent than the parents are to each other and are shown closer to an adult than to siblings.

3. The parents are placed on the same level and are relatively the same size.

4. The adults are larger than the children.

5. Betty's position, as pictured, allows her an unobstructed "view" of the entire system, including a clear view of the couple system.

6. There are five evident sub-systems in the family—the parental system (placement of symbols by themselves on same level), the systems formed between a son and a parent (proximity), the sibling sub-system (smaller size), and the system formed by the brothers (same symbol).

7. Betty's brothers comprise a sub-system that is hierarchically above Betty and although they are equidistant from Betty, they form a subsystem of similarity that excludes Betty.

8. The greatest distance between symbols within a subsystem is the distance between siblings, who are positioned equidistant from each other.

9. All the male figures are represented by four sided figures.

10. The female figures are similar in that they are different from the males, both being non-four sided figures.

11. Betty is represented by a shape that is most different than others in the family, being the only one that is not composed of lines.

Inferences, relative to intimacy, that might be drawn from this representation are:

1. Betty's models for intimacy could inform her that there is more closeness between parents and children than there is between the adults. This might result, in her adult life, in her putting a relationship with a child more important than her relationship with an intimate partner. She could easily justify making decisions about intimacy with a partner less important than her responsibilities as a parent, *even when they may not be justified.*

2. Betty could have a meager foundation for peer interactions as she seems to be excluded from the sibling sub-system.

3. Betty might have an inherent affinity for hierarchical sub-systems because they are familiar to her and she

has learned how to function within them. Since hierarchy in an intimate system between partners is counter indicated and a precursor for a breakdown in intimacy (see discussion later in this chapter), Betty's intimate systems are quite possibly fraught with the potential for difficulty. Betty might *naturally and unawares* seek out individuals with whom she is inherently superior or inferior, and then find herself with unsatisfied intimacy.

A relationship history revealed that Betty had always been the youngest person in her classes in school. She was a precocious child and was allowed to enter first grade at four and a half in an educational system that did not adhere to current age limits. While she was capable of being on a par intellectually with her classmates and sometimes superior to them, she was not socially the peer of five and six year olds. In addition, her family frequently prevented her from participating in the common social events of her classmates, claiming that she was too young for them. Betty's adolescent boy friends and her girl friends were most frequently from a social class that was less than her family's standards. These situations created opportunities for her to be the one who was superior, and at the same time allowed her to be different and distant from the rest of her family. Her brothers generally chose dating partners and friends from among the group that received parental approval.

Betty's interactions with her brothers were restricted. Her parents sent the brothers to private school and Betty went to public schools. The rationale was that as a precedent in the ethnic make-up of the family, it was more important for the males in the family to be given advantages that would help them in future endeavors. The females were expected to be wives and mothers and therefore not in need of special educational privileges. This led to Betty's experience of being inferior and driving her choices of peers to those who were inferior. She abjectly rejected friends whom she deemed superior to her in education, social class, or sophistication.

True to form, Betty married Jack when both were young. Jack was considered to be a poor choice by her family as he was not up to her skill level in several areas nor was he of her social class. She became a mother within a year of the marriage and proceeded to have four children, sons, in rapid order. From those who knew her, she was commended for her mothering. However, within fourteen years, it was evident that the marriage was in serious trouble.

Betty had continued her education on a part time basis through her child-raising years resulting in both her bachelor degree and a master's degree. Jack, with a high school diploma, showed evidence of resentment about her education and the employment possibilities they presented. His dissatisfaction with her growing competencies and his family's expressed displeasure at a wife who "didn't know her place," eventually led to instances of violence between them that was not revealed to outsiders.

Jack's family diagram is pictured below in Figure 3:

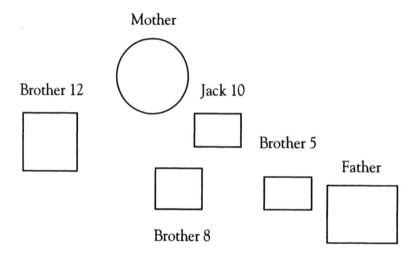

Figure 3: Jack's Family Diagram

Interactive patterns that can be hypothesized in Jack's family diagram together with inferences that might be drawn from them are listed below (again, in practice this list would be generated by the couple in their process of self discovery):

1. The mother is placed higher than everyone else in the family, an indication of her possible power and influence.
2. Children are positioned between the adults. This could be seen as indicative (from Jack's perspective) that the marital pair had no free access to each other.
3. Jack (the second son) is pictured closest to his mother with no unobstructed view of his father,

which could indicate that he was prevented from having direct access to his father.

4. A son is closer to his father than the father is to his wife, possibly indicative of father attempting to substitute closeness with this son for intimacy with his wife. The same could be true of mother and the couple's three other sons.

5. The eldest brother is almost equal in size (possibly denoting relative influence) to the father and is largest of siblings.

6. The eldest brother is most distant (and possibly most isolated) from other siblings.

7. There is an identification (similar shapes) among the males in the family.

8. The sub-systems appear to be mother and three oldest sons, father and youngest son, mother and Jack (proximity), and mother and 3rd son (placement). Most noticeable by its absence is the lack of a discernable sub-system between the marital pair.

Examining the two diagrams side by side with the premise that individuals without awareness replicate patterns of interaction that were "learned" in their families of origin, it is possible to hypothesize that the marriage between Betty and Jack had inherent flaws from the beginning. In both families it was "natural" that parent child systems were closer (more intimate) than couple systems. From an assessment of the current dyadic system it was apparent that Betty had fallen into the place of Jack's mother in the family schema; she was superior (in education, family of origin status, class and sophistication) to Jack. Betty's expectation that she was inferior to the males in her family probably resulted in her confusion about her place as a wife when coupled with her felt experience of superiority to Jack. Neither individual had models for intimacy among cross gender peers that could serve as templates for successful relationships.

When presented with these two diagrams, Betty and Jack were struck by the differences between their families and without prompting were able to articulate the following:

Jack; I think our family now is almost exactly like mine was when I was a child!

Betty: (With tears choked back) I'm shocked! I'm just like your mother.

Jack: I never realized how little my parents had to do with each other. Looking at that picture reminds me of how my father was always working and my mother took charge of everything. She really left him out of things and he didn't seem to do anything to make it different. I didn't ever hear him complain, but then why would he, his gambling habit would have been exposed!

Betty: You seem to leave most of the family decisions up to me and then complain when I don't consult with you about things. My mother decided the important things of the family too, but that doesn't show in my diagram.

The couple spent several sessions focusing on the awarenesses they gained through a therapist-guided examination of their diagrams. Primary among these were those related to intimacy. Both agreed that they had different ideas of what intimacy "should" be like between married couples and were unsure if they could, or wanted to, find a common ground. Their goals for their life as a couple and family were diametrically opposed and within a relatively short time, the oldest son had an incident that involved the judicial system that further polarized the couple. Eventually they separated and later divorced.

Notes on Using the Diagram Exercise

This projective device has the potential for uncovering factors that are unaware to the individuals and potentially *either* growth producing or a rationale for defensiveness and obfuscation. The outcome depends on the therapist's integrity to the process of discovery. Therefore the therapist should not interpret the diagram to the couple, and the therapist must not lead the couple.

This exercise is a device of self and relationship discovery with the therapist functioning purely as a facilitator of the process. The therapist begins this process by presenting the directions clearly without further explanations. Typically individuals ask about using all symbols, only some of the symbols, or attempt to obtain more specific directions. The therapist must not elaborate on the directions. To do so would risk contamination of the results. However, it is important that the therapist resist elaboration in a casual manner.

Once the diagrams are complete the therapist can use the following directives to elicit awareness:

"Talk to each other about the similarities you (both) notice in your drawings."

"What is evident to you about the relationships between symbols? Which symbols are closest to which other symbols? Which symbols are available to have contact with another symbol?"

"Describe the relationship between symbols that seems most outstanding to you."

"Which set of symbols seems familiar (or foreign) to you both?"

Often couples will make few statements about the drawings at the outset. Presenting the couple with a copy of the drawings, without any directive to do "homework" allows the couple to continue at home what was begun in the session. This further supports the dyadic boundary and allows the couple to make connections in private. Often they report significant results in subsequent sessions.

The Factors of Intimacy

Equality – the non-hierarchical relationship

This couple's story illustrates one of the most significant obstacles to intimacy – the inherent inability to establish and maintain a relationship of equality. The dyadic system is predicated on a foundation of relating as peers. Intimacy is possible only to the degree that a non-hierarchical relationship exists between the individuals in the couple system. This is complicated by the fact that many individuals have no experiential models for this despite the tendency to look within a peer group for an intimate partner.

Age, of course is the most relevant facet of peer relating. Individuals tend, in general to have social relationships with others within their broad age group. This tends to follow the premise that the sibling group is an individual's first entry into peer relationships and all the skills of peer relating are established within this group.

Of course, the sibling group is further embedded within the family system. Individuals who have the advantage of being raised in a cross gender sibling system learn the idiosyncratic nuances of males and females. Those who emerge from a single gender sibling group often find the intricacies of the opposite gender incomprehensible and foreign.

Carl Whitaker (1989) claims that an age difference between a couple of more than fifteen years represents an age difference that approximates a generational chasm. When this is coupled with Minuchin's "rule" that two generations should not share a subsystem, it is evident that this age difference constitutes a non-peer system.

There are obvious reasons for the attraction between individuals with a significant age difference. In addition there is a "honeymoon" period that belies the difficulties that generally emerge as the relationship "ages." The inherent fault in non-peer systems is that in time they become parent-child systems, where one individual takes on parental functions that the other must accept and reciprocate. In the throes of romance, this dynamic is common and functional. Solicit-ness is driven by a desire to please the partner. In the company of passion, these behaviors are benign. However when aspects of self-functioning are foregone in an effort to maintain this state, discontent begins to brew. Eventually as the dynamic becomes a fixed mode of interaction, the dyadic relationship deteriorates into a parent-child mode. When this occurs, there is a resulting discontent with sexual relating. Beneath the surface, despite the overt "complaints," is an emergent, albeit unacknowledged, clash with the incest taboo. Sexual pleasure is inherently unallowable between parent and child. As the hierarchical structure of the dyad becomes irrevocably fixed, all facets of intimacy are disturbed.

Non-equality fosters a lack of respect and caring. Decisions made from a position of superiority without adequate negotiation or input, present a situation of potential resentment. When this is a pattern of relating learned in the family of origin, it is experienced as a *natural way of being*. It also carries with it the inability to exercise non-hostile personal power and the potential for an intentional or unawares annihilation of self..

Intimate relating requires the participation of whole "selves" – an ability to merge with another without loss of self. When one partner engulfs the individuality of the other, there is a loss of ego boundaries, and intimacy is impossible.

Functional disputes are those that have as a core principle the need and desire for change *in the relationship*. This only occurs when there is an absence of fear of annihilation; when there is a presumed assurance that each partner will be heard and can speak with equal influence. Generally children "absorb" their parents' means of negotiating or "fighting" and tend to replicate this pattern as adults. In a hierarchical dyadic system, the fight, or dispute tends to be centered on the dynamic of getting even, not in the manner of revenge, but rather as an attempt to equalize the power and influence. Frequently there is an unacknowledged withholding of intimacy as an act of getting even that *does* function as revenge or punishment. When any of these patterns become entrenched, intimacy recedes and often it is impossible to regain it.

Differentiation from Family of Origin

Murray (1978) claimed that the process of differentiation is the major developmental task of young adulthood and one that coincides with choosing an intimate partner. When what is termed "the ties of intimacy" are stronger (albeit different) than the intimacy between the couple, there is a foreboding of difficulty.

In looking back at the diagrams of Betty and Jack, the inherent learned loyalties are revealed, and the foundation for disturbances in intimacy becomes obvious. Betty appears, in her diagram, to be distant and relatively differentiated from her family of origin. She is most different in her shape, most distant, and unfettered by other family members. However, these are some of the very factors that may keep her from differentiating. There is an overt illusion of independence that overshadows her inability to be dependent or inter-dependent, a necessary component of intimacy. And in effect she is the pivotal individual in her diagram making her further entrenched in family dynamics. Her plight, one that interferes with her capacity for intimate relating, is that she appears to be "free" while experiencing herself as inextricably tied.

Jack, on the other hand is clearly hemmed in by family members with no obvious "escape route." His ability to be self-differentiated is further hampered by the lack of a close relationship between the parents. The closeness between Jack and his mother approximates the closeness that would be more appropriate between adult partners and his emotional and physical leaving could be viewed as an act of disloyalty. In any regard, his choosing an intimate partner would remove him from closeness with his mother if successful. In actuality, one of Betty's complaints was that Jack put his mother and his family of origin needs above those of their family of procreation and she expressed the sentiment that her input into family decisions was always less important than his mother's opinions. Jack's emotional ties to his mother and his loyalty to his family precluded his ability to establish and maintain intimacy with his partner. Their *mutual* inability to master differentiation, contributed significantly to their ineffectualness at attaining satisfactory intimacy in their dyadic system.

A Foundation of Similarities to Support Superficial Differences

The intimate system requires a combination of similarities *and* differences. The interaction of the polarities leads to a creative tension that keeps the system lively, rich in possibilities for personal and relationship growth, and fosters flexibility. However there needs to be a balance of similarities and differences to allow for *both* stability and fluidity.

Intimacy originates in a foundation of real and perceived similarities. Some basics in this general category might include race, religion, family values, educational level, financial status, anxiety tolerance, intimacy tolerance, level of differentiation, and responses to threats. Some of these factors are obvious, while others are inextricably illusive and only emerge in interaction. The basic similarities allow the couple to operate from a generally compatible base of decision-making. There is an intrinsic understanding of where each is "coming from" in actions and reactions. Further there is an acceptance of a way of being and an unspoken understanding of motives.

Looking once again at Betty and Jack, their similarities are obvious. They are both Caucasian, Catholic, southern European in ethnicity, and from families in generally similar financial situations. One core difference is in educational levels. Betty's parents both had earned high school diplomas and valued education while neither of Jack's parents graduated from high school nor did they value higher education. Another basic difference was in family values regarding closeness; Jack's family existed in a climate of maintaining concrete similarities. All family members were expected to vacation together; work in the family business; and drive similar make automobiles. Betty's family operated more individualistically. Siblings got together infrequently; differences in life style were supported; and following family rituals was a matter of individual choice.

The function of a foundation of similarities is to support *superficial* differences. Some of these differences are in the realm of leisure time activities: choices of friendships, vacation possibilities, and the other similar non-essential factors. These are the differences that make individuals and their relating interesting and fresh. In Jack and Betty's relationship their differences took on the aspect of chasms that led them too far apart to be intimate. Their core differences overshadowed the basic similarities and interfered with their ability to maintain intimacy.

One or two significant differences alone do not necessarily become a precursor of disturbances in intimacy. They cannot, however, be incorporated by the couple as superficial differences or overlooked as a potential breeding ground for a rift in the fabric of intimate relating. Such differences take on more significant importance when they occur in conjunction with other basic dysfunctions.

Commitment

Intimacy must be grounded in a nourishing environment that is circumscribed by commitment. The degree to which there is an absence of conditions of commitment, is the degree to which intimacy can't flourish. Unconditional commitment carries an expectation of endurance *despite* difficulties. It is a relationship where there is an understanding that all disturbances are co-created and that these difficulties present opportunities for growth and change rather than a path to dissolution of the relationship. It is only with this implicit assurance that intimacy can develop and flourish. Individuals who come from a background of parents who have engaged in serial pseudo-intimate relationships have little *natural* tolerance or understanding of this level of commitment. They enter so-called intimate relationships with a myriad of conditions that are often unspoken but which lurk in the background available for "use" should intimacy become threatening or threatened. The most common of these conditions is infidelity, which frequently is an inherited pattern. Children learn, either inadvertently or directly, that a spouse has "cheated" and therefore the relationship had to end. There is no understanding of the rift in intimacy that was a precursor of the search for intimacy that resulted in the breach of spousal boundaries. The infidelity is a *result of* a lack of intimacy rather than *the cause of* an absence of intimacy.

Both Betty and Jack seemed to come from families of origin where there was a presumed level of commitment. Both sets of parents remained married. However, upon closer examination, it was apparent that this was simply a blind following of religious tenet. There were no options so conditions were unexpressed or unacknowledged. If transgressions occurred, they were buried and "punishments" meted out as a natural function. However, it was telling to note that all of Jack's siblings were in second or third relationships and one of Betty's brothers was divorced and living at home with the parents. It might be speculated that these parents projected their unacknowledged conditions onto their children who unwittingly constructed relationships where the parent's unexpressed dissatisfactions could be enacted. The assumption cannot be made that an unconditional commitment was operational in the parents' marriages based solely on longevity.

Intimacy cannot thrive without commitment. Further, passion and romantic love are not synonymous with intimacy. When the element of commitment is intentionally added to the dyadic relationship the opportunity for enduring intimacy is manifest. However intentionality is not a given in relationships. It often is considered non-romantic and thereby avoided. It is, nevertheless, vital and essentially the main focus of therapy when complaints or concerns about intimacy are presented.

Summary and Conclusions

The infrastructure of intimate relating in a couple system is established in the family of origin. It exists without notice and frequently gets overlooked by therapists working with a couple. Furthermore this family of origin template is a factor that cannot be accessed with any degree of reliability by routine probes. Often the couple is patently unaware of the possibility that they could be following in their parents' relationship footsteps and loyalty may make them resistant to being forthcoming if they do possess awareness.

The majority of couples who elect therapy or who have been recommended to get therapy have complaints about the relationship that can be translated to dissatisfactions with their intimate relating. The presenting problems will rarely include the actual word intimacy, but rather the difficulty with intimacy is embedded within the complaint. The most obvious is the transgression against relationship rules; the extra-marital affair. Others include the over simplistic report that he/she doesn't love the other any more. Some of the most common grievances that speak to the disturbance of intimacy are the inability to communicate with each other; the lack of time spent together; the continuous "fights;" and difficulties with time, money and family members. Each of these reproaches has an element of intimacy at the core, or the difficulty results in a disturbance in intimate relating.

The form and function of intimacy must be flexible enough to withstand the changes that take place over the life cycle. Being intimate as a newly connected couple is entirely different than maintaining intimacy in the face of aging and illness. Intentionally planning for time and space for intimate relating, when the demands of raising children and managing work and finances places constraints on a relationship, requires different skills. Negotiating the changes in closeness and distance inherent in being a couple alone before or after the advent of children presents unique challenges. Throughout these different stages, the couple progresses most often without any specific skills *other than those they acquired unknowingly in their families of origin.*

The exercise that formed the skeleton of this article is both a respectful and an awareness facilitating intervention that is helpful to the couple and the therapist. It is also a useful tool for supervisors of therapists working with couples to assist them in eliminating unaware projections originating from the therapist's family of origin. The authors have used this exercise over twenty-five years of working with couples and supervisees. Once the diagram is completed, the subject is asked to tell "stories" about their family of origin. The anecdotal reports fill out what he/she has noticed in his/her family diagram.

The capacity for intimacy is formulated in the primary systems in the family; the relationship between parents; the subject's relationship with each parent; and the subject's relationship with siblings. These, taken together, emerge into a template of intimacy that follows individuals into their adult relationships. Each of these primary relationships has input into the factors of closeness and distance; power and control; dominance; functional and dysfunctional dependence and independence; sexual activity; skills of negotiation and compromise. Taken together these factors make up the complex fabric of intimacy and are irrevocably tied to family of origin learning.

The more understanding an individual has of the complexity of intimacy and the roots of intimacy within the family of origin, the more possible it is to attain and sustain intimacy. Intimacy is the connecting tissue between individuals, the essential force that brings couples together and either sustains their relationship or lacking it, drives them apart. Intimacy cannot, or should not be taken for granted, or expected to flourish without direct and intentional attention. Without considering the family of origin factors inherent in intimate relating, the couple and therapist are entering the area of change lacking armor and tools.

References

Bowen, M. (1978). *Family Therapy in Clinical Practice*. New York: J. Aronson.

Minuchin, S. (1974). *Families and Family Therapy*. Cambridge, MA: Harvard University Press.

Whitaker, C. A. (1989). *Midnight Musings of a Family Therapist*. New York: Norton.

Editor's Note:

Jenny and Brian O'Neil have been an important part of the Gestalt therapy community in Australia for over two decades. Co-founders and co-directors of the Illawarra Gestalt Centre (near Sydney), they have worked together as therapists and trainers for many years and have forged a program and a presence that is based on relationship, connection and support. Over the last ten years they have extended their presence to the international community with their intimate involvement in the Association for the Advancement of Gestalt Therapy (highlighted in particular with Brian's presidency and their influence on the 7th and 8th International AAGT conferences) and with their subsequent international teaching and training.

Here in this chapter, they present their intuitively bright conceptualization of a couple as a "oneness," which allows a deeper appreciation of couples' experience and development. In addition, they eloquently share with us how their ability to struggle with, distill and appreciate their own complexity as a couple has honed their ability to be with, understand, and respond to the couples they see in therapy—a lesson and inspiration for all of us in how to harness the experiences of our own relationships in the service of our work.

9

• • • • • • • • • • • • • •

The Secret Life of Us
Brian & Jenny O'Neill

There is a secret language of intimacy. A dance between belonging (connecting) and shaming (disconnecting). A dance done particularly by couples, which is so intimate that it makes working with couples in psychotherapy distinctly different.

There is a saying, that to *know* something is knowledge, to *understand* it is intelligence and to *live* it is wisdom (Swedenborg, 1992/1768). How do we as a couple therefore know, understand and live this secret language—as therapists with other couples and as a couple ourselves.

You might suppose that as therapists, we have an advantage in this dance of connecting and disconnecting. Yet for all couples, therapists or not, our knowledge and intelligence about shame and belonging do not solve or heal everything—far from it! So much of this life as a couple must just be lived. It is bigger than the two individuals living this. It is different and more than the sum of the parts—this is the sum of us, the secret life of us.

These experiences of connecting and disconnecting, of

shame and hurt and love that Robert talks about, are directly lived experiences beyond words, which become embodied in our very being. We want to speak of this embodiment, with ourselves and in our work with others. This is therefore a very intimate space we write from as a couple.

Many of our initial discussions for this chapter were while driving through the Adelaide Hills, which is a particularly picturesque area in Southern Australia, and over lunches in our favourite café, the Organic Café, at Stirling. The richness of our environment is somehow figural and reflective of our process of developing the chapter for this book, as is the sense of our writing for the first time *as a couple.*

Much of this is our *ground* in writing about couples therapy and shame, our own experiences both personally and professionally as to how we not only teach and do therapy but also live this secret language of intimacy. In particular we want to connect with the material Robert has provided, with a focus on the dance between shame and connectedness and the importance connectedness has in a field experience, and for us as a couple.

But first let us present a theoretical ground for how we envision couple experience.

Field Theory of the Couple

The self is a system of contacts in
the organism/ environment field.
(PHG, 1951/1984, p. 228)

This description of self is similar to that found in many religious and spiritual texts describing the experience of self as indistinguishable and a priori **at one** with the all that is. PHG goes further in stating:

> Let us call this interacting of organism and environment in any function the "organism/environment field;" and let us remember no matter how we theorize about impulses, drives etc., it is always to such an interacting field that we are referring, and not to an isolated animal. Where the organism is mobile in a great field and has a complicated internal structure, like an animal, it seems plausible to speak of it by itself—as, for instance, the skin and what is contained in it—but this simply is an illusion due to the fact that the motion through space and the internal detail call attention to themselves against the relative stability and simplicity of the background (p. 228)

The implication of what is being said is stark and challenging —*our sense of a separate self is an illusion.* An illusion or at best an experience of self built with the functioning of a separate ego which develops later. As the child starts to discriminate *self* and *not self,* such ego functions develop. As the child learns to language reality, this language of self and ego becomes the personality—the way in which we describe ourselves in words and concepts.

This definition of self in PHG allows us to move beyond the separateness of ego to experience the many selves which arise, come into being and then fade into the ground. From this definition of self we can say that when two people become systematised in their contact with each other, they are a self—a couple.

This concept is found originally in Gestalt Psychology, as outlined by Wertheimer (1925/1997), and the relationship to the later work of Perls, Hefferline and Goodman is clear. The basic, fundamental formula for Gestalt theory, as outlined by Wertheimer, presents a description of the field and the self in a way which is consistent with the work of both Smuts (1926) and PHG:

> There are wholes, the behavior of which is not determined by that of their individual elements, but where the part-processes are themselves determined by the intrinsic nature of the whole" (p. 2)

The connection to the later theory of Gestalt therapy is evident. The organism is part of a larger field of organism and environment. In a statement predating the concept of self in Gestalt therapy, Wertheimer describes the meaningful, functioning whole of a group of people, such as South Sea Islanders as being a "self," an organism. In such situations he states that the "I" of the person rarely stands out alone and it is the wider organism of the group which exists.

The Couple as One

The concept of the couple as a self in the organism/environment field offers a unique aesthetic to enter into contact with a couple in therapy. In essence we realise the couple we are contacting is *One Life*. They appear as two people of course, but in the view of the couple as one, a richer fuller tapestry emerges. This is at the heart of the original work by Martin Buber, *I-Thou*, and provides a lens with which to understand his deeply mystical and personal style of writing.

As Buber (1958) writes:

> The human being is not a He or She, bounded from every other He or She, a specific point in space and time within the net of the world; nor is he a nature able to be experienced and described, a loose bundle of named qualities. But with no neighbour and whole in himself, he is Thou and fills the universe. (p. 8)

While describing the separate person as "whole in himself" (an individual), Buber paradoxically at the same time tells how she is a Thou which fills the universe. The person is both a separate identity and connected to all there is in a mystical fashion. Her separate identity also fills the universe and is more than the individual personal nature of "self." Such an experience of self is most fully experienced in an enduring sense as part of a couple.

> By the very recognition that there is something larger present in the therapy situation than just the sum of the total of the individuals physically there, this is already a recognition of the "more than personal." (Hycner, p. 97)

This description is particularly relevant to the couple, where there is indeed something "larger" present in the therapy situation than the sum of the two individuals physically present. There is a presence of that which is "more than the personal" —the couple self.

Hycner also describes the Hasidic story of the holy sparks which initially are "All that Is" shattered into holy sparks, which are separated and contained in all things, yet remain the common source of wholeness. To paraphrase this in couples therapy, the self as a couple (containing the holy sparks), provides the experience of two separate beings (sparks) nonetheless connected in the experience of coupling (wholeness). It is this connection we experience as the "between." We want to emphasize this is a view of the couple *both* as a "oneness" (a self) and also as two individuals in a field. As we shift to experience the couple as an ongoing "self" then a wider view opens to therapy and spiritual life.

Note that within the therapy context in working with a couple, there is a greater self still, of the therapist and couple together. However for the purposes of this work our focus will be with the self of the couple.

The Spiritual Life of the Couple as One

There are elements in all religions which in some form honor the spiritual nature of the *couple*. This sacred aspect of coupling is most beautifully described in the writing of Kahlil Gibran (1924):

You were born together,

    and together you shall be forever more,

You shall be together when

    the white wings of death scatter your days,

Aye, you shall be together

    even in the silent memory of God.

But let there be spaces in your togetherness.

And let the winds of the heavens dance between you.

                        (p. 16)

Gibran in these brief lines describes the essence of a struggle that is perpetual in all couples work—the challenge to allow "spaces in your togetherness." This experience of "oneness" of the couple can challenge the core of our separate sense of self. For while we may tolerate the oneness in love making or in intimate states of looking after each other as a couple, yet in such union there is also a heightened potential loss of ego control. This challenge to our experience of a separate, individual self may cause us to rebel and struggle as we enter into the developmental processes of coupling.

As Erv and Miriam Polster (1973) state:

Contact is not just togetherness or joining. It can only happen between separate beings always requiring independence and always risking capture in the union. At the moment of union, one's fullest sense of his person is swept along into a new creation. I am no longer only me, but me and thee make we. (p. 99)

The couple is the new creation and the Polsters describe the challenge of *risking capture* in the union, *gambling* with the dissolution of individuality and *wagering* our independent existence. This attention to *both* the individual's and couple's experience of self, and the tension between each are, to us as therapists, very important. It is particularly well articulated through shame theory and the field theory definition of the couple.

When people reach the stage of their lives that they start looking for a partner, they have accumulated various amounts of what Robert calls ground shame and have developed creative adjustments that incorporate their ground shame into styles of connecting (Lee, 2004; Wheeler, 1991).

Here is where the concept of a couple's "oneness" or "self" provides a lens that offers a unique view. This mix of life experience and beliefs as well as the individual's yearnings for connection become an integral part of their couple "oneness." In this way a couple's "oneness" includes their mutual sense of disconnection as well as their longing for and accumulated skills of connection.

As connection is the reason for coupling in the first place, connection and a desire to grow are the major driving forces operating in couples developing "oneness." However, in their "oneness," couples can find themselves moving toward connection, *or* they can find themselves reinforcing in each other the sense that connection is not possible. This is because, ironically, moving toward connection may activate the couples sense of the necessity of disconnection. Hence the couple's joint underlying beliefs, embodied in their styles of connecting, contain taboos that require a disowning of aspects of self in order to "belong." Simple examples of these manifest as "If I am strong I will be loved (but not if I am weak)" or "I can never fully trust another with ALL of me."

The degree to which a couple individually "disown" aspects of themselves in order to be a couple, is a benchmark of the degree to which a couple may seek support and therapy in order to re-align these creative adjustments to become more authentic as a couple and as individuals.

Such experiences are paradoxical as is the change that is engendered, and it helps to know at some level that this couple is a self. This creates an awareness for therapists not only of each individual but to the couple as a whole. This knowingness can lead us to understand that there are two "realities" at play here—the reality evident to our senses of the two people and the more subtle reality of the self of the couple. Each has a clear aesthetic to our senses, yet our phenomenology needs to be educated and developed to look for the signs of two individuals acting also as a couple. This is found in glances, in touch and in words, yet the phenomenological mind set which is only fixed to observe the separate self of the individual will be "blind" to these sensory figures—to all intents and purposes this reality of the couple self is "invisible."

As we become aware that this other reality exists, we can begin to relate to the couple "self" as well as the two individual selves which are present. We may ask the couple questions and look at what the couple actually does in physical space.

For example we may see the couple come in and say they are both nervous yet willing to be here. They might be sitting far apart.

> One person may start by saying: "the problem we are here with is that you hurt me by your being with another."

> The other may respond: "I didn't mean to, but you never listened to me."

> They may move further apart. The first person might say: "you hurt me and I don't want to be with you anymore, I can't trust you"

> And the other person may likewise say: "I am very bloody angry at you... how long do you want me to suffer for this, I just feel like leaving you again."

As each individual expresses these polarities of contact and withdrawal, we may start to notice paradoxically the couple itself has moved much closer physically and emotionally and is in full contact and not at all about to even consider leaving the room at this point.

So we as therapists become aware that there is a couple "self" here in the room. As we work from this awareness we may start to ask simple questions of the couple *as a whole* and not just each separate individual, such as:

> "what moves you apart here as a couple and what brings you closer together"

It is in such contact with the couple as a "self" that the therapist truly begins to engage in couples work, and not only works with the two individuals as a couple, but also the couple *as a whole*.

The shift to a profoundly simple process of working with each individual and the couple as a whole, is not only a theoretical construct. This is a lived reality which challenges our very notion of being a separate self. The experience of being a couple calls out the illusion of the separate self divorced from the wider field. This state of reality may be frightening to many, as we may feel we are losing our selves, risking capture in the union, as the Polsters described it.

As poets, mystics, musicians and artists will attest, this is not an easy state to maintain. And as a minister once told us—"marriage is like your relationship with God—we struggle to get closer."

So to repeat :

There are wholes, the behavior of which is not determined by that of their individual elements, but where the part-processes are themselves determined by the intrinsic nature of the whole (Wertheimer, 1925/1938, p. 2)

There is the couple, the behavior of which is not determined by that of the two individuals that make up the couple, but where the individuals themselves are determined by the intrinsic nature of the couple.

The Way Our Theoretical Principles
Inform Our Practice

There is a practical interest in seeing the couple as an organism *in itself*, as well as attending to each individual person that make up the couple. This perspective of the couple as a oneness allows for a new dimension of work to enter into the therapy. The impact of *the couple* on the individuals can be considered, and this is, in our view, a very important element of the work. We can work experience of "coupleness" through simple phenomenological questions such as: "what is it like to experience yourselves as a couple and not just two separate people?"

Dialogically we can make statements about how we see them as separate people and how we experience them as a oneness, a couple. We can also dialogically share our own experience of being a couple.

Further, there is an openness to experiment with this experience of being a couple and two separate people through experiences which present in the therapy room. With one couple who came in it was clear they were very much in tune with their separate individual natures and so we asked if they were metaphorically sitting on the sofa today or two separate chairs. They laughed and said they were sitting on the chairs and this became a useful reference to language the field of the couple and the individual selves.

Paradoxically, this focus on the couple can and does bring out the individual resistance to being a couple. This risk of losing individual "self" in the union of the couple "self" also highlights the subtleness of working with these individual and couple realities.

There are times for instance when the couple is not ready to be received as a couple and share this intimacy and may be more aware of their individuality. In such instances the couple wants to be attended to individually and this is often particularly so at the beginning of therapy. Each person has a sense of their issues, their hurts and their sense of shame and distress. When this is particularly potent the couple may need individual therapy at the same time as the couples work to gain support or may even need to consider individual work first before coming together in the couples work.

As an example, one couple was recently being offered to experience themselves as a couple and to work on the issues as a couple but they insisted, gently at first and then more strongly, that the issues from previous marriages needed to be worked on separately. They could sense that these were individual issues which were getting in the way and they wanted the separate space to deal with this so as not to make this blurred with how they were as a couple.

Some clinicians might argue against this approach and say that these issues are connected, yet this would not be hearing the couple's sense of their need. At the very least we can be willing to experiment with the couple to find out what works and to take our lead from them.

In some instances the couples we have worked with have such a high degree of distress, stemming from sexual abuse, domestic violence or the like, that individual work seems clearly indicated before working as a couple, yet in other cases couples are ready enough as a couple to work on these issues together.

Determining whether we focus the work with the couple on two separate individuals, *or* whether we work with the couple as a self, would seem to be best judged by the couple themselves. It is perhaps more the role of the therapist to be able to match her approach to the stage and pace of the couple.

For first time couple therapists it may be difficult to shift from the individual paradigm to a focus on the couple as a "oneness," because individual personalities are what our culture celebrates. To look at two people in couples work and see that they are also a gestalt—a whole—a self, is at times almost the totally opposite experience for the therapist—like being asked to believe the world is round when standing in the middle of a vast open plain.

As we become more experienced in staying with the couple reality, as well as that of the two individuals, we are able to be aware of paradoxical polarities in this dance of connecting and disconnecting, of shame and belonging. It helps as a couple to have experienced the polarity of wanting to belong *while at the same time* needing to disconnect through shame. This is particularly so when our sense of vulnerability does not include the possibility of connection.

In therapy we find there are times when we are interested in working with both people and the couple as a whole, and other times when the focus is with one of the individuals in the couple and the other withdraws more into the background and attends.

This offers the possibility for the therapist to work for a session with one of the people in the couple on family of origin issues, with the other present. This helps them to appreciate the genesis of these shame cycles and contact styles. This further confirms our understanding of the usefulness of at times working first with the individual process of one of the couple so that they can, as a couple, come to understand and support each other better. Working this way allows the individual work to stay in the context of the couple.

When a couple fights

One of the useful things Robert does in his workshop is to provide his own personal experiences of being a couple. He shares the effects of shaming and then not shaming and the differences this has brought to their relationship. This seems very valuable to couples.

Fighting is a secret shame for many couples, both in respect to what they believe others might think about their relationship and in how they themselves hold the possibilities of their relationship.

At times these fights may be very hurtful, painful and tiring and lead to a sense of disillusionment. Understanding how such fights can be a normal part of couple life and acquiring a capacity to hold the seemingly paradoxical intense feelings of intimacy, which includes both the love and the war of being married, can be extremely supportive to couples. We have found this to be true in our own relationship.

Similar to the Buddhist perspective that life is suffering, an analogy we use in sharing this with other couples, is that the ups and downs of marriage and coupling is like the weather. You cannot totally escape rain; yet you can look for the part of the country that has climate that suits you. For us as a couple these fights are a journey to different climates of our marriage, many of which are developmental, particularly with the rearing of children. We have been at stages of our relationship where even beyond any counseling, we sat in despair and reached for each other. In connecting through the pain of fighting we have experienced the strength of working as a oneness when needed.

It is these sorts of experiences that help sustain us in working with other couples, providing hope and supporting our ability to look for *resilience* and *growth* in the chaos of disorder and the struggle of fighting. It is not uncommon that when we have sufficiently held a couple through the "heat" of one of these encounters, supporting them in an unshaming manner in the face of the expression of strong negative emotions towards each other, that they have returned to the next session rather sheepishly reporting that they found themselves making mad passionate love with each other that night. This is clearly a paradoxical shift that we treasure.

In our own relationship, the times when we fight usually occur when, as a couple, we feel under resourced—overly stressed, with insufficient support in our personal and/or couple world. If one of us is feeling more supported we can muster the resources to "be there" for the other and this further develops the life and strength of us as individuals in our couple, as well as our couple as a "self."

For example, there was an incident where we began arguing while walking through the Botanic Gardens and one said to the other: "I just need you to *not* fight and just be here for me for a while—hear me without needing to defend or respond with your stuff."

This was a clear request, a yearning, which was more potent than the process of shaming and fighting. It spoke to our strength as a couple. It made sense, intellectually and emotionally. We learned as a couple to "dance" with this and "take turns" at points when we recognized the other had a deeper need.

Paradoxically, attending to the "good of the individual" can at the same time be attending to the "good of the couple" and vice versa. It is a matter of holding, as a couple, the combined needs of us as individuals. When this is done, when we each have an ear to our combined needs, then in fact attending to the "good of the individual," within this relational context, turns out to be attending to the "good of the couple," with the reverse being true also.

Along this line, it has been important for us as a couple to learn about the roots of each other's vulnerability. One way this has occurred is with seeing our partner working in workshops. This has allowed us to stand back and watch the elements of our partner's life unfold before our eyes and see patterns of shame and disruption which are informed by our family of origin experiences. This has supported each of us being able to stand beside the other in our process at times and note the effect we have on each other when it is *us* who are fighting or disconnecting.

Couples handle varying degrees of shame, struggling and disconnecting with each other—some times passively, at other times actively. Many times this is a combination of old patterns learned from our family of origin as well as the unique creative adjustments we have developed as a couple.

At times our mothers and father are also speaking inside our heads as we struggle and at times they are speaking *with* us to the other. This is a very subtle and insidious dance of our past experiences in our families of origin shaping our present relationship.

Robert demonstrates so well in his workshops how these "resistances" are not just solitary states which happen within the individual and in the individual's response to another. These creative adjustments and patterns also *connect* with the patterns of the other partner and form a *new* symbiotic pattern that happens *between* the couple. This begins to have a "life of its own" as part of the couple system of contacts.

This system of contacting which involves hurt, shame and pain becomes part of the self of the couple and can overwhelm the individuals who make up the couple.

Many couples who argue report these feelings and thoughts and identify strongly with these embodied patterns of shame. Robert has demonstrated the universal nature of this as a "lived experience" in his workshops. It is paradoxically comforting, connecting and supporting for the couple to hear that these reactions are common and that all couples experience this to one extent or another.

There are other couples who come to therapy and who present with little or no expressed anger with each other. They tend to withdraw or ignore each other or even live separate lives. They tend not to share these yearnings and may instead develop the sense of either or both being a victim.

In such cases the nature of shame is apparent in a disconnection and sometimes manifest in only one of the people in the couple being identified as "ill." In more intense examples of this pattern there is evident retroflective behavior, such as depression, drug addiction or self harm.

The Art of Therapy

The presentation of this to couples, like drawing the shame attack itself on the white board can be, in our experience, a very helpful process for the couple. This supports them in beginning to understand the hidden elements in their interactions, which in turn enables them to experiment with these repetitive patterns from a position that is more in tune with their underlying yearnings. They begin to see these as patterns of behavior, learned usually in their family of origin and further developed by themselves, and they can more quickly "catch" and explore the underlying connective value of the these patterns of contact as the patterns come into action.

This process tends to move couples toward a fuller awareness of their yearnings for each other, which may be camouflaged or guarded. As such it can also expose instances in which people have coupled or remain coupled for reasons other than an interest in one another. For example, with one couple, who were bitterly fighting, we drew a red square and a green square on the whiteboard. We explained red is the things you say that interrupt a sense of cohesion or connection between the two of you. These could be things that you intend or that the other finds to be attacking, insensitive, self serving or the like. Or they could be things that are said, perhaps unknowingly, without sufficient support for the other to take in. Green is the things you say that create or continue a sense that the two of you are on the same team. These could be things that are intended or received as loving, playful, appreciative—engaging/enlivening for the couple in some way. These could even be things that are said in anger, if they are said with sufficient support and said at a time when the other is capable of receiving the anger. The important element here is that both partners wind up feeling that they are valued members of the same team. Summing up, we offered:

> It seems like you are used to speaking to each other from the red square, as if you are not on the same team. Would you like to try speaking from the green square, imagining that you are on the same team, for one minute and see what happens?

This couple could not do one minute. We inquired about the red square and its attraction and what emerged was that the red square had a bitter yet sweet taste of revenge for both of them. Beyond this they found that they had little interest in one another. While they had loved each other at one time, they had both suffered too much emotional damage at the other's hands and were living solely to get even, as if they were addicted to this bitter pill. When they eventually became fully aware that they could not recover their interest in one another they decided to separate rather than continue to hurt each other and this in itself was the paradoxical beginning of the couple looking after each other.

In general in working with couples, putting these experiences into simple colors or metaphors can be of great benefit. It helps couples to notice the difference between a couple and an individual reality in fighting. When a couple shifts from the individually isolating position of being "done to," with its concomitant experience of being hurt and its employment of offensive or defensive, shame driven strategies to attack or avoid the other, to "we're angry" or "we are getting red," then this simple shift allows the couple to ally with one another. This in turn enables them to notice and to deal with the hidden element in their interaction—namely that one or both of them are off-balance in some manner. Acknowledging, as a couple, the support that one or both need(s) brings a sense of mutual compassion, which often unlocks their creative resources in the service of dealing with whatever issue they are facing.

The Story of Us is the Sum of Us

Much of what we have written so far stems from our accumulated knowledge and understanding of couples. Yet, as the saying with which we started this chapter foretells, the degree to which this represents a wisdom is directly linked to the degree to which we have lived our own story as a couple.

The ability for us as a couple to endure and learn from these intense states of love and pain, shame and belonging, connection and disconnection prepares us as therapists to be with other couples, intimately and in the moment. These *experiences*, and not just our understanding or knowledge, link us appreciatively with other couples. For a couple in therapy, having contact with another couple, who also struggles and who loves, helps the couple feel less shamed and to become interested in and respectful of their own process. Correspondingly, we have found that our theoretical map must include a trusting in and listening to the lived wisdom of the couple we are with.

Melnick et al. (1994), in their work on ethics and Gestalt therapy, talk about the Gestalt therapist having difficulty with the "intimate moments" of interpersonal work as opposed to the traditional insight oriented approach of the Freudian school. They state one of the ethical practices of this work is to be able to stay with the client while the client experiences intense emotional states. We extend this to ethical practice with couples—being able to stay with couples in these intense intimate moments, often filled with uncertainty and chaos, is crucial to the success of therapy with couples. Not surprisingly, couples can move into an intense emotional state much quicker than individuals, as the presence of the therapist "invokes the actual" (Van Dusen, 1975) of the couple as a lived entity and not just as a story to be told in therapy.

At this point the therapist, by his/her presence alone, in being able to tolerate this degree of anger, hopelessness and shame, can provide a de-shaming or normalizing effect. In this vein, it is the ground of the therapist's *own* relationship and the degree to which he/she has learned to tolerate and has lived through such difficult yet intimate moments in his/her *own couple relationship* that can paradoxically support the couple at this point.

Our ability to talk about and discuss our own patterns as well as the patterns of couples we see, adds significantly to our ability to meet and stay with the *experiences* of the other couple and offer hope and support for their wisdom as a couple.

We know, understand and experience that in moving through these difficult times in being a couple, there is something bigger than us individually that we can count on. We can count on us as a couple. The sum of us.

This experience of the couple as a connectedness parallels that which many mystics have described in their striving to experience the *more than* the individual *me*. This sense of losing oneself and becoming part of something bigger is not limited to such esoteric concepts. This connectedness may be found in everyday reality: in painting a picture, in playing music, being in nature, cheering on your football team, or being in a family gathering and laughing.

At times we find ourselves congratulating or supporting our "couple-ness" after an argument. We note the hard times we have experienced and the stresses we have endured. We have discovered we are "worth it"—worth the struggle to get close, the dance of connection and disconnection, of shame and belonging. We *are* the "it"—a rich mixture of fighting and loving; gardening together and arguing over house renovations; raising children and feeling hopeless and frightened when they are seriously ill; fighting with them as they develop and grow and "take on" mum and dad; and sitting tearfully with them as they share their hurt and pain.

At this point we are proud to be the couple we are and the family we have become. As we look back on early days and remember the birth of children and how young we once were, we see we have developed individually and as a couple and each of the struggles has been part of bringing us here, to where we are now.

We continue to face life together, held together in the secret intimacy that is US—the secret life of us as it exists with all couples—the sum of us.

References

Buber, M. (1958). *I-Thou*. New York: Scribner Books.

Ellis, W. (Ed.). (1938/1997). *A Source Book of Gestalt Psychology*. The New York: Gestalt Journal Press.

Gibran, K. (1924). *The Prophet*. NY: Alfred A. Knopf, Inc.

Hycner, R. (1995). The Healing Relationship in Gestalt Therapy: A Dialogic—Self-Psychology Approach.

Lee, R. (Ed.). (2004). *The Values of Connection: A Relational Approach to Ethics*. Hillsdale, NJ: GestaltPress/The Analytic Press.

Melnick, J., Nevis, S., & Melnick, G. (1994). Therapeutic Ethics: A gestalt Perspective. *The British Gestalt Journal* 3:105-113.

Perls, F., Hefferline, R., & Goodman, P. (1951/1984). *Gestalt Therapy: Excitement and Growth in the Human Personality*. London: Souvenir Press edition.

Polster, E. & Polster, M. (1973). *Gestalt Therapy Integrated: Contours of Theory and Practice*. New York: Brunner-Mazel.

Polster, E & Polster, M. (1999). *From the Radical Center: The Heart of Gestalt Therapy*. Santa Cruz, CA: GestaltPress.

Smuts, J. (1926/1999). *Holism and Evolution: The Original Source of the Holistic Approach to Life*, (edited by S. Holst). Sherman Oaks, CA: Sierra Sunrise Books.

Swedenborg, E. (1768/1992). *Conjugial Love*. New York: Swedenborg Foundation.

Van Dusen, W. (1975). Invoking the actual. In J. O. Stevens (Ed.), *Gestalt Is* (pp. 75-86). Moab, UT: Real People Press.

Wertheimer, M. (1925/1997). Gestalt theory. In W. Ellis (Ed.), *A Source Book of Gestalt Psychology* (pp. 1-70}). New York: The Gestalt Journal Press.

Wheeler, G. (1991). *Gestalt Reconsidered: A New Approach to Contact and Resistance*. New York: GIC Press/Gardner Press.

Editor's Note:

Frank Staemmler is a long time master clinician, trainer, editor, and writer. His presence radiates a quite warmth, competence, and humility. To meet him is to feel seen and supported, to be at ease, and to feel the possibility of adventure. In the following chapter he brings his keen intellect to the task of defining and addressing the subject-matter of Gestalt therapy with couples.

In Staemmler's words this consists of three elements: (1) The process of clarification of the respective *responsibilities* of the partners for their own behavior and for their attribution of meanings. (2) The work regarding the partners' awareness of the fundamental fact that the other views the world and operates from her or his own *independent* system of constructions; this includes a mutual informing the other partner of one's own meanings as well as an interest in the partner's meanings. And (3) the elaboration and/or discovery of joint meanings, which are built upon mutual knowledge of and respect for the individual meanings of the partners and which also integrate them into a system of meanings on a higher, relational level. With an understanding of these elements in mind the couple therapist can direct her or his attention more clearly to the interaction and relationship of the couple.

10

• • • • • • • • • • • • •

Joint Constructions:
On the Subject Matter of Gestalt
Couple Therapy, Exemplified by
Gender-Specific Misunderstandings
with Regard to Intimacy

Frank-M. Staemmler

In marital counseling, the approach used by many caseworkers has been to treat the individuals involved in terms of their respective neuroses, with change in the marital relationship coming as a by-product of improved individual adjustment. This method really amounts to treating an individual who happens to have a marital problem rather than treating the marriage relationship itself. (Gehrke & Moxom, 1962, p. 253)

Relationships are at a different conceptual level than individuals and may not be reduced to assessments of individual characteristics. (Sroufe, 1989, p. 97)

Almost thirty years ago I had my first therapy session with a couple. I must admit that I felt a strong relief when it was over. Never before in my then short career as a psychotherapist had I experienced that much powerlessness and discomposure: after they had taken their seats it took only seconds for them to engage in a furious fight in which one word led to another without any discernable moments of hesitation or consideration. I had a hard time getting my stunned mouth shut again—not to mention my desperate, although futile, attempts to snatch an opportunity to enter the hurried play.

When the session was over I felt completely frustrated. I did not feel that I had contributed anything helpful, but even more discouraging, I did not see how I could have been more effective. So for a few years I decided that working with couples was not one of my strengths. For the time being I restricted myself to individual work. By way of what today I think was a helpless rationalization I took the simplistic and individualistic point of view that healthy people entertain healthy relationships, and if the relationships are ailing the partners need to do individual therapy (maybe in the presence of the other) in order to limber up for their relationship.

Several years later I began to see things differently. Not only had I become a little more courageous, but also I had the experiences of facing and overcoming problems in my own partnership. [1] For me the most important aspect of those

---

[1] My companion in life, Barbara Staemmler, has contributed to this article in many respects: First, she is the one with whom I have learned, through our relationship, about being partners over the past thirty-six

experiences was that my immediate impressions of myself during a conflict or an argument with my wife taught me an irrefutable fact that—sometimes much to my regret!—it was not my independent, individual me that was involved; no, it was some "me-in-relationship" who felt and acted in ways that, to a certain extent, were beyond my individual control and pretty much influenced by my wife's conduct and our joint situation.

It started to dawn on me that maybe a kind of *couple* therapy which deserves that name is not just a pooling together of two individual therapies. Perhaps it can more appropriately be seen as a *different* task demanding a *different* vantage point of the therapist and, most likely, *different* procedures as well: Maybe a relationship is ailing because partners hold on to their respective individualities in a way that is detrimental to their relationship or, to put it more extremely, because the partners fail to let go of attributing highest priority to their individualities and hence are unable to transcend these priorities to the detriment of achieving an integration of their individualities into their relationship.

Tragically, this would mean that ailing relationships both suffer from and prolong the efficacy of the individualistic paradigm rampant in Western societies:

The fundamental propositions of that paradigm . . . are:
1) that *the individual is prior to relationship, and exists in*

---

years, second, she has participated equally in numerous joint discussions which have enabled clarification and understanding of many important experiences in our therapeutic work with couples. and third, through her critique she has helped me to describe the female perspective in this article more adequately.

some essential way apart from relational context and connection, and 2) that *relationships themselves are therefore secondary, and in some sense less real than the individuals who enter into them* . . . (Wheeler, 2000, p. 53, italics in original).

The individualistic paradigm is one possible way of interpreting the world—one, but not the only one. The world, human "nature," and interpersonal relationships can also be understood in different ways. Specifically, the *meaning* people attribute to their world is the decisive dimension. And meaning is *created* by people. But it is not only individually created, to a large degree it is also created by the culture into which one is "thrown." Human beings already experience their world in such a way that their interpretation as well as their language and culture, which strongly inform their interpretation, are ". . . *already present in the very experience itself*" (Lakoff & Johnson, 1980, p. 57, italics added).

Robert Lee's initial chapters in this book present the reader with numerous examples for this basic human reality. Not only does it start with the story of Janet and Henry who obviously see the same set of "facts" in very different ways. Moreover, throughout his presentation Lee deals with the "*secret language of intimacy*," that is with the way women and men interpret intimate situations and relations in ways that at least in parts escape their awareness. In my view, Lee's work with couples focuses essentially on their—implicit and explicit—meaning-making.

One fact, of course, is no secret: Women tend to create different meanings than men. This is not, as a famous book title would have it, because *Men Are From Mars, Women Are From Venus* (Gray, 1992). As far as I know both men and women are terrestrial creatures and their respective gender-specific ways of meaning-making depend to a large degree on their earthly physical and social environments. However, their differences in making sense of their worlds result in severe frictions sometimes. For those couples who seek a therapist and find me at such times, I now have a clearer idea of how to support them than I had thirty years ago.

In what follows I will lay out some of my thoughts that have helped me find my way through the still sometimes difficult work with couples.

What to Work On?

In my search for a better orientation I looked at the gestalt literature on couple therapy. However, I did not find a satisfactory answer to the one question that was most important to me: What exactly is it that a couple therapist needs to work on? Of course, some writers have already commented on this question, e. g. Harman: ". . . the relationship is the patient" (1989, p. 73), or Zinker: "The Gestalt therapist focuses on the space where they meet and not on their internal space" (1992, p. 294). Greenberg and Johnson provide a more comprehensive characterization:

> In . . . marital therapy, it seems more useful, rather than focusing on innate predispositions, to focus on each partner's position as it is evoked and maintained by the

immediate emotional experiences in the relationship and the responses of the partner. The behavior of the partners is then viewed as a function of the relationship rather than in terms of personality traits or psychopathology. (1988, p. 77).

I fully agree with these statements; they certainly point to the essential, non-individualistic dimension in the work with couples. However, I did not find them precise enough to help me direct my attention clearly.

As I have said before, the accentuation of the focus on the relationship and on the interaction of the couple appears extremely important to me. Traditionally, the work with couples (similar to the work with groups) very often was practiced in the style of *individual* therapy—as I practiced it myself in former years (see my introductory quote). Perls's (1973, pp. 150ff.) work with couples clearly is an example of this style. Nevertheless, in my opinion it makes a big difference, if you work with one partner in the presence of the other or if you work with the *couple*.[2] Sometimes, individual work with *one*

---

[2] Family and systems therapies have also tried to overcome the individualistic bias. They did so by addressing themselves to "the system" or to the rules that determine a family's communication. This never appealed to me; it felt much too impersonal. Although I do not follow an individualistic idea as the nature of being human, I still want to relate to *persons* in relation, i.e. to couples, not just to systems. This position is informed by Martin Buber, who in his famous discussion with Carl Rogers said the following:

. . . the concept "person" is seemingly very near to the concept "individual." I would think that it is advisable to distinguish partner in the presence of the other can be an important and useful aspect of couple therapy, given that it represents a minor part of the work and given that it refers to *both* partners to a fairly equal degree. Addressing therapeutic interventions much more often to one partner than to the other is equivalent to attributing the responsibility for the partnership difficulties primarily to one partner or even to making one partner the scapegoat of the relationship. In no case the work with the couple can be replaced by work with the individual partners.

I will demonstrate this by the example of the pattern of male/female gender misunderstandings: In my therapeutic work with couples, I have repeatedly encountered a certain problematic constellation in the relationships between my clients and their partners, which was related to how they approach each other sexually. In the following, I intend to describe this problematic constellation in more detail for several reasons: First, it seems to be important in itself because of its great frequency, and second, it can serve as a useful example of a certain *pattern* of conflicts between partners—a pattern which also occurs in many different contexts. And third, this pattern offers an opportunity to deduce some general thoughts about gestalt couple therapy.

---

between them. An individual is just a certain uniqueness of a human being. . . . But a person, I would say, is an individual living really with the world. And *with* the world, I don't mean *in* the world—just in *real contact*, in real reciprocity with the world in all the points in which the world can meet man. . . . I'm *against* individuals and *for* persons. (1965, pp. 183f., italics in original)

But first I will give you another example in order to illustrate a distinction, which will become essential for my argument below: the distinction between the *behavior* of a person on one hand, and the different *meanings* on the other hand, which may be ascribed to her or his behavior by *either* herself or himself *or* by other people. This example also has to do with gender.

English Girls and American Boys

In the introduction to their book *Pragmatics of Human Communication* Watzlawick et al. (1969) report the following story:

Among the American soldiers who, during the war, were stationed in England, there was the wide-spread opinion that English girls were very easily accessible sexually. Strangely enough, the English girls held that the American boys were excessively impetuous. Research revealed what follows: Courtship behavior—from the first encounter to sexual intercourse—consisted of about 30 different steps both in England and in America, but the sequences of these steps differed enormously in both cultures. Whereas in America kissing appeared fairly early, i. e. around step 5, kissing in typical English courtship behavior was observed fairly late, i. e. around step 25. In practice this meant that an English girl who was kissed by an American boy... had to decide whether to break off the relationship or to surrender sexually. In case she chose the latter alternative, her American lover found himself confronted with a behavior which for him did not at all fit into this early stage of development and which in his view appeared rather shameless. Of course, the solution of such a relational conflict by the partners is almost impossible, since those culturally conditioned ways of behavior and sequences are most of the time completely out of awareness. What does come to the minds of the respective individuals, though, is the vague feeling: the *other* does something wrong. (Watzlawick et al., 1969, p. 20—italics in original)

What took place between the English girls and the American soldiers, can be divided into two levels, first the level of *behavior* (the kissing) and, second, the level of the *meanings* which the participants ascribe to their behaviors. On the behavioral level, the English girls and the American soldiers display a behavior, i. e. kissing each other, which to the external observer appears identical. On the level of meanings, there is a big difference, though: The American feels he is behaving in accordance with step five of the pairing scale, i. e. relatively reserved; at the same time the English girl puts his kiss on step twenty-five of the scale. According to the meaning she ascribes to his behavior, she thinks her lover is a daredevil; thus, she finds herself being confronted with the question, whether to set up a limit immediately or to go to bed with him right away.

The American, who subjectively is still in an early phase of pairing (step five), does not ask himself this question yet. He thinks, he has to take twenty more steps, before the decision will be made of whether the two are going to make love or not.

Perhaps, in spite of some resistance to the speedy development of things, in the meantime the girl has made up her mind to surrender to the courtship activities of her supposedly very impetuous lover. Now, he faces a behavior that fits step twenty-six of his scale, instead of step six which he expected next. Very surprised he takes his chance and arrives at the conclusion, that English girls are pretty uninhibited.

Reducing the kissing situation as described above to the elements that are important for my following thoughts, it can be schematized as such:

	English Girls	**American Boys**
Behavior	kissing	kissing
Meaning	step twenty-five	step five

Table 1

The example shows the far-reaching consequences that may arise, if people do not communicate thoroughly about the meanings they attribute to certain behaviors. Very often in relationships an important precondition for such a communication is missing, i.e. the awareness of the fact, that any behavior never carries a specific meaning in itself, but that the meanings are always ascribed to the behaviors by people in a specific culture.

Sex for Intimacy or Intimacy for Sex?

Similar to the intercultural differences between English girls and American boys, at least in Western culture, a wide-spread gender-specific difference exists in regard to the meaning that many women ascribe to their sexually approaching a man on one hand, and the meaning that many men ascribe to their sexually approaching a woman on the other hand. In many cases the following simplification contains a greater or lesser amount of truth: The man needs sex for intimacy, the woman needs intimacy for sex (see McWhirter, 1992).[3]

If a woman and a man behave in accordance with this pattern without being aware of it and without communicating about it, problems are very likely to occur. Since this pattern in my view plays a specific role in many heterosexual[4] relationships and frequently exercises a great influence, I will describe it in more detail trying to make comprehensible which problems may ensue from it.[5] I make three presumptions, however:

1. This pattern does *not* exist in *every* partnership (be it only for the reason that the man is submissive to the

---

[3] Of course, some couples establish the reverse constellation. And in some relationships an exchange of roles takes place from time to time.

[4] In some homosexual relationships the same constellations can be observed.

[5] In the following paragraphs I draw heavily on an article by Bergner and Bergner (1990), in which I have found a very precise description of my own observations.

woman or *vice versa*[6]);

2. in any partnership which exhibits this pattern one can find unique nuances which are characteristic only for *this* partnership;

3. in *every* partnership additional interactive patterns can be observed which will modify, complicate, super-impose, as well as intensify or weaken the effect of the pattern in question.

Having said this I can go on: For many women sexual contact with a man functions as a *medium*, within which they can *express* an *already existing* feeling of intimacy or belonging that needs to have grown before in a more or less non-sexual way. Only after intimacy has developed on the basis of joint activities or experiences (such as going out for dinner, having a meaningful personal conversation, or dancing together) these women find a clearly sexual approach adequate. On the basis of an intimacy that has evolved from non-sexual activities they can feel seen and confirmed in their uniqueness. Thus they can be relatively sure, that it is not "just their body" the man wants, but that they are being appreciated and loved as a *whole* person.

For many men, the reverse connection is valid: For them, a sexual approach can appear adequate at a much earlier point in time, since they regard it as a means to *induce* a feeling of

---

[6] The "hunger for acceptance" can seduce some women, which Wardetzki (1990) likes to call "female-narcissistic", to conform with the needs of men to an extent, that makes those needs look as if they were their own. And some men completely obey the expectations of their wives, because they think they cannot bear their fear of being left.

closeness and belonging, which they have *missed* before and which they desire as much as many women. If a woman gives in to their sexual advances, they experience being loved and appreciated not only physically but as a *whole* person. There is actually no better way for them to feel valued and confirmed by a woman, since now they can be relatively sure, that they are wanted not only as a "good fellow."

In principle, we are dealing with a situation which is very similar to the one between the English girls and the American boys as described by Watzlawick et al. Using the same scheme as above, the situation can be characterized as such:

	Men	**Women**
Behavior	sexual approach	sexual approach
Meaning	means for inducing a not yet existing feeling of intimacy	expression of an already existing feeling of intimacy

Table 2

Problems

It goes without saying that neither the "male" nor the "female" perspective is better or worse than the other; they are just different. This difference in itself does not have to be a problem in a relationship. However, to the degree to which the gender-specific differences are effective in the partners without being conscious, understood, accepted, and worked through in terms of a joint solution, serious difficulties *between* the partners may develop. As long as the general condition of the partnership is satisfying for both partners, such difficulties are usually of minor importance or are not even experienced as such, because within an overall positive atmosphere the partners receive a sufficient amount of personal confirmation by each other. With this essential precondition given, the different ways of experience do not become disturbing.

When the relationship is going through a phase of a major distance or even crisis between the partners, very often the impact of the gender-specific differences on the partners increases strongly. The husband will be likely to try to resume the disturbed connection with the wife by an attempt to approach her in a sexual way; thus hoping to re-establish the intimacy with his partner and his feeling of being loved and confirmed. The wife, possibly, experiences his behavior as impersonal, inadequate, or as a violation of her boundaries, since she misses the conditions under which sexual contact is acceptable to her. Maybe she thinks her partner does not really love her and assumes that he is only interested in her body or wants to (ab-)use her for his purely physical satisfaction.

He may take his rejection by her as an offence, since for him it probably means a rejection of his whole person, a degradation to the level of sexually neutral "fellow" as well as a frustration of his desire for closeness. Given these feelings, it will not be easy for him to comply with her needs for extensive talks, or other non-sexual joint activities. Sometimes, he can see the expression of her needs solely as blackmail, or some other sort of power-ploy, by which she employs sexual contact as a reward, if he gives in to her needs, or the withdrawal from sexual contact as punishment, if he does not subjugate himself to her will.

Once the vicious circle of offences and mutual misunder-standings is established, it is not a long way to the point at which both partners, while trying hard to handle their frustration and to maintain their self-esteem, pin each other down to devaluating stereotypes: He calls her "frigid," and she blames him for only wanting to fuck. They are entering an infertile dialogue; he occupies the role[7] of the demanding "topdog," she plays the refusing "underdog." These roles can be played quite readily, for they are in accordance with the gender-specific social stereotypes which both of them are very likely to have introjected long ago. Sooner or later, they see each other and themselves as reduced personalities, whose wholeness is both not perceived by the other anymore and not felt by the individual:

> Reality is continuously being constructed in a way that it confirms the constructs about the partner. If one is not able to change the partner according to one's own ideas, one at least wants to protect one's own self-esteem by presenting oneself as the victim of the partner. (Willi et al., 1992, p. 78)

---

[7] By "role" I mean ". . . a pattern of behaviour emerging from the person's own construction system rather than primarily out of his social circumstances" (Kelly, 1955, p. 68). I will return to this quote later.

Frequently, what remains is an endless chain of mutual reproaches and accusations with both partners making strong efforts to reserve the seemingly preferable role of the victim for herself or himself and to put the partner into the shoes of the perpetrator—if they do not withdraw in resignation and avoid contact at all. Just like the English girls and the American boys, each of them thinks the *other* is wrong.

Both for the practice of couple therapy and for my attempt to grasp the subject-matter of couple therapy in this article, it is important to keep in mind that we are dealing with a *pattern of interaction*, within which the wife gets caught by one role and the husband by the other. Only within this pattern of interaction they are captive in the clutches of these roles, out of which they cannot free themselves easily. Therefore, I do *not* regard it as an *individual attribute* of the husband to be demanding and pushing, and I do *not* see it as an *individual character trait* of the wife to be refusing. Instead, both of them display a very small portion of their entire behavioral range, and both of them suffer from the fact that they communicate in a way that binds them to a certain role and leads to a restriction of their flexibility and differentiation, which both for themselves and each other is extremely unpleasant and sometimes even humiliating.[8]

---

[8] This restriction can be understood as a regressive process (see Staemmler, 1997), which is evoked by both partners both within themselves and in each other.

Responsibilities

At this point I will try to make a first theoretical step of abstraction. I refer to the above-mentioned difference between the level of behavior and the level of meaning.

Within couple therapy one is first confronted with the behaviors of two persons, i.e. the behavior of the husband and the behavior of the wife. These two elements are related to each other: Behavioristically speaking, the behavior of the husband serves as a stimulus for the wife, and the response of the wife serves as a stimulus for the husband, and so on in a circular fashion. Thus, the behavioral level of the interaction can be depicted schematically as follows:

1st Scheme of Interaction

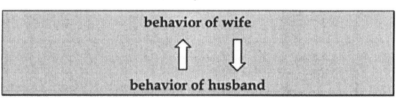

Legend: The partners interact in a circular manner. They react mainly habitually to certain behaviors of the respective other, thereby exhibiting relatively stereotyped ways of behavior. The behavior of the respective other is regarded to be instructive for one's own behavior.

Obviously, this representation of the interaction is extremely simple. Nevertheless, it captures a couple dynamic frequently present in critical situations. Very often couple members define themselves as if they were thinking of themselves as conditioned

mice: "I only do such and such, *because you* do such and such."
—"*If you* would change, I could change . . ." Within this
model of interaction, only the *behavior* of the partner exists, and
this behavior is held to be *causally determinant* for one's own
behavior.

> Distressed couples exhibit extremely rigid, repetitive
> patterns of interaction that can be easily identified most
> of the time. These patterns or 'cycles,' so called since the
> actions of each spouse are at once a stimulus for and a
> response to the actions of the other, are automatic,
> immediate, and self-perpetuating, with the couple taking
> habitual positions in each interaction. (Greenberg &
> Johnson, 1988, p. 73)

These habitual positions and their afore-mentioned
representation are insufficient to make an interaction
understandable, and they are even less useful as a model of a
relationship between partners, since "the relationship.... is made
up of the observed interactions *as interpreted*" (Stern, 1989,
p. 55 —italics added). Further information must be gained by
appreciating the limitations of this representation of couple
interactions. We need to take into account that "humans are
cognitive and affective beings, and human interactions center
on interpretation and meaning" (Sroufe, 1989, p. 98; see also
Mead, 1934). Only the attribution of meaning makes a reaction
of one partner to the other comprehensible and makes it become
a *relational* event. But it takes place within a person's mind;
unlike behavior it is not directly accessible for external

observers, including partners.

In other words, the wife *interprets* the behavior of her partner in her personal manner by ascribing a certain *meaning* to it. The husband, in reverse, does the same in his special way. Both of them do not react to the behavior of their respective partners, but to the *meaning* which they *ascribe* to it. The wife attributes a certain meaning to the behavior of the husband; then she reacts to that meaning. The husband attributes a certain meaning to the behavior of the wife; then he reacts to that meaning.

This interlink, i.e. the ability to add meaning, is the ground on which human freedom and responsibility rest. Human beings cannot plead to be primitive organisms which are nothing but victims of their reflexes. In human beings, a certain psychological stimulus does *not automatically* elicit a certain response. Humans can and do exercise some influence on their interaction patterns, since they are the *authors* of the respective meanings which they attribute to the behaviors of others.

Thus, the behavior of one person *cannot cause* the reaction of another, it can only *trigger* it. "This interaction is not instructive, for it does not determine what its effects are going to be. Therefore, we have used the expression 'to trigger' an effect" (Maturana & Varela, 1987, p. 96).

2nd Scheme of Interaction

the meaning the wife ascribes
to the behavior of her husband ⇨ behavior of wife

⇧ ⇩

behavior of husband ⇦ the meaning the husband
ascribes to the behavior of his wife

Legend: For the most part the partners are aware that they attribute meanings to the behaviors of the other, that they themselves are responsible for these attributions, and that their own behavior results from the meanings they have attributed to the other's behavior. The vertical, big arrows indicate the interactions between the persons, the horizontal, smaller arrows indicate internal processes within the persons.

If the husband who, in the scene described above, receives a refusal of his sexual approach from his wife, feels she does not accept him as a whole person but only as a good fellow, *he* is the creator of, and responsible for, the attribution of this meaning and the emotions that may arise from it.[9] Conversely, it is the wife's authorship and responsibility, if *she* ascribes a meaning to the sexual approaches of her husband that make her feel devalued as a whole person and used as a means of his drive satisfaction.

At this point I want to contradict a wide-spread opinion according to which the distribution of responsibilities, as

---

[9] Even in case the woman thinks of him as only a good fellow and tells him so, he is responsible for the meaning he attributes to that statement.

undertaken in the paragraph above, equals statements such as: "You are to blame, if you feel like that. You don't have a right to be angry with your partner. It's just *your* problem!" I do not agree with this. An individual who takes responsibility for her or his view and feelings, does not only have a *right* to see things her or his way and to feel in her or his way. Moreover, s/he *can* see things only in her or his way—and that does not have to be a problem. Of course, s/he has the opportunity to change her or his mind, in case it appears inadequate or unsatisfactory to her or him. But the view that results from this change of mind again is *her* or *his* view. "The world, as we see it, is always exactly this: the world *as we see it*" (Richards & von Glasersfeld, 1987, p. 215 —italics in original). The view of each person is, therefore, always original in some respect—including both its advantages and its disadvantages. As Goethe said: "That which isn't original, isn't appealing, and that which is original, always carries the shortcomings of the individual with it" (1976, p. 179).

For the external observer it is obvious that the mutual attributions of meanings by the partners frequently contain a great many implicit assumptions. Both of them impute to the respective other that her or his behavior would spring from the same intentions as would be the case, if s/he herself or himself would behave as such. The woman assumes that the psychical processes in the man, which she cannot directly observe, are the same as the ones that would take place within herself, were she to act the same as he. Were she to approach him sexually, at that given point in time, she could only do so without a feeling of closeness. For her, this would mean to regard her husband as an exclusively sexual being, toward whom she did not experience the kind of closeness that, actually, for her, is a precondition for any sexual approach. Since for her a sexual approach means an expression of an already existing feeling, she would be behaving as if there were an intimacy, which she does not experience at that moment.

The man assumes that the woman has the same feelings that he would have, if he would refuse a sexual approach. From his perspective, a sexual approach provides a chance to induce a feeling of closeness towards her, which he does not yet experience at that given point in time; the refusal of a sexual approach means that he is not interested in intimacy, because for instance, he does not like the woman or does not find her attractive. At this point, he assumes the same of her and correspondingly feels refused.

Both of them lack the knowledge and/or the consideration of the meanings, which the behavior of the other has for her or for him. "Unresolveable partnership conflicts are based not only on unconscious collusive entanglements, but also on the fact that the partners cannot understand each other, since they construct their respective realities in different ways without knowing it" (Willi et al., 1992, p. 81). The husband ignores the meaning which the behavior of his wife has for his wife; he fills the gap of his ignorance with his own meanings which he attributes to her. In the same manner she does not take into account, which meaning the behavior of her husband has for her husband; instead, she attributes her meanings to him.

With the preceding paragraphs I have come to the point, at

which a first subject-matter of the therapeutic work with couples becomes clear. It consists of *the process of clarification of the respective responsibilities of the partners for their own behavior and for their attribution of meanings.* I purposely say "*process* of clarification of the responsibilities," because this work normally constitutes a more or less continuous therapeutic *process*, in the course of which the partners slowly discover their implicit attributions and thereby, step by step, discover their own responsibilities.[10]

As a result of these discoveries, in most cases *differences* become salient at first. By "differences" I mean the distinctions between what on one hand can meaningfully and usefully be assorted to the one person, and what on the other hand can be assorted to the other person. The clarity of such differences between people forms an essential precondition for a satisfactory relationship. I suppose that Fritz Perls (1973) intended to underline this with his famous "gestalt prayer":

I am I,
And you are you.
I'm not in this world to live up to your expectations.
And you're not in this world to live up to mine. (p. 140)

---

[10] Of course, the work with couples is based on the same gestalt therapy principles as the work with individuals, i.e. responsibilities are not distributed by the therapist in a pedagogical or moralistic way; instead, the therapist supports the partners in making their own discoveries. This support is especially necessary when the partners are off-balance, because in those situations they are more likely to be incapable of forming meaning in a way that acknowledges their respective authorships.

Thus, working on this first subject-matter of couple therapy has a quality of differentiation and sometimes even separation; here things are divided and separated which had been mixed and confused before. Frequently clients find this process also relieving and clarifying. Their wish for closeness, however, still remains unsatisfied.

Complications

I will return, now, to the entanglements of the couple. It would have been good for them, if they had already asked for therapeutic help and did not wait for their problems to worsen. Given that their respective responsibilities had not been clarified and their misunderstandings continued, an escalation of the difficulties between them would very likely occur: The man will tend to intensify his efforts for inducing closeness and runs the risk of feeling increasingly dependent on the obligingness of the woman; he may put even more pressure on her. ("If you would only make love to me again, everything would be much easier.") For her this may give rise to even more defensiveness, since his behavior triggers her suspicion that he does not really mean to address her as a person. ("You only want to make love, but you don't really love me.") If they do not manage to find a way out of this vicious circle of mutual frustrations, insults, and the resulting feelings of hopelessness and anger, in extreme cases very destructive reactions may occur.

Men who tend to abuse their physical power are most likely to lose control at this point of the escalation. Here, the abuse of physical power against the woman serves several functions: First and foremost, it enables the man to reverse the up-down relation, within which he, in the final analysis saw himself in the inferior, dependent, and powerless position. Second, he can seemingly free himself of the unbearable feeling of insult by quickly switching from the role of the passive victim to the role of the active perpetrator—while, of course, using the justification of being the *true* victim. Third, the abuse of his physical power provides a possibility to release some of the aggressive energy that he has accumulated during the previous interaction. In case he succeeds in keeping up his control, violent verbal eruptions may serve the same purposes; frequently they contain strong devaluating statements about the woman.

Sometimes he seeks liberation from his agony by having an affair. This can be understood as a delayed and deflected form of aggression, which promises to satisfy both his need for revenge and his need for sex. All of the husband's ways of aggression-release mentioned above are apt to reinforce his wife's tendency to withdraw; they even seem to, subsequently, justify her previous withdrawal.

Once the situation between the partners has escalated like this, they usually have lost any awareness of their joint need for interchange, closeness, and intimacy. Both of them view the situation only from their respective perspectives, and neither of them is able any longer to adopt a *third* point of view, i.e. to become a steward of the *relationship*.

> . . . no one speaks for the *couple*. Each person stands up
> for his/her idea, refusing to give up one's pride, or lose
> face. Who is watching out for the marriage? They are so

busy being stuck in their pride, they simply forget that an argument is an effort to solve a problem. . . . They have not incorporated a sense of marital pleasure and pride as a source of their own esteem. (Zinker, 1983, pp. 24f. — italics in original).

Very often the third perspective has to be introduced into the partners' awareness from outside, for instance, by the therapist. It is only from this third perspective that the individual behaviors of the participants, the subjective right of which from their *individual* perspectives does not need to be challenged, can be recognized and experienced as counterproductive. They are counterproductive, because measured by what may emerge as the *joint needs* of the couple and related to their joint interest in the *relationship* the individual perspectives clearly have the character of *avoidances*. The individually determinated behaviors have become parts of a *joint* interactive pattern, within which both partners do not get what they actually want. In addition, their relationship is increasingly endangered, since they are moving further and further away from forming a mutual supportive system and a community which provide *quantitatively more* and *qualitatively different* opportunities for the two of them to satisfy their needs and to grow personally than they would be able to without the other.

Individual Systems of Construction

In other words, the partners relate to each other on the basis of personal constructions, within which their *common* situation is represented preponderantly from their *individual* perspectives and, thus, insufficiently. This is exactly what the second scheme of interaction was to describe.

2nd Scheme of Interaction (repeated)

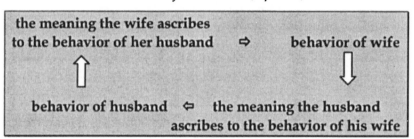

The meaning, for instance, which the behavior of the wife has *for herself*, cannot be found here, because they remain irrelevant for the behavior of the husband. As I said earlier, for the husband the behavior of his wife takes on the meaning that it would have for him, if he would have behaved that way, and *vice versa*. Their respective constructions and meanings do not contain the constructions and meanings of their respective partner; their constructions are not *relational* constructions. Each of them is playing a *role*, which is primarily ". . . emerging from the person's *own* construction system rather than primarily out of his social circumstances" (Kelly, 1955, p. 68—italics added). The "social circumstances" are the results of the fact that both partners always interact *in relation* to each other, and, indeed, their relationship always includes their personal constructions of their respective partner, only by which her or his behavior can be understood. But it is exactly this fact that is ignored by both of them.

Of course, one can empathize with the temptation to act like this: Initially, in relation to each other, both spouses can be regarded as external observers, who, on the basis of their observational data, cannot have any certain knowledge about each other's internal processes. They are able to observe their partners' behaviors, but this is not a sufficient precondition to also *understand* them. The gap of understanding can be bridged quickly by them by inserting the meanings one can deduce from her or his own system of construction. So, the behavior of the partner at least makes *sense*. It is part of the frequent tragedy of marriages that this method of making sense, though is does seem to save time, is counterproductive in most cases. Therefore, in couple therapy the following discovery must not be avoided: "Ultimately it is complex constructions or views of reality that govern interactions in couples and need to be changed in order to change these interactions" (Greenberg & Johnson 1988, p. 21).

From this follows the second important subject-matter of couple therapy, i.e. *the work on the partners' awareness of the fundamental fact that the other views the world and operates from her or his own and independent system of constructions.* From this system each partner deduces meanings which s/he ascribes to her or his own behavior and which in most cases deviate from those which the 'observing' partner attributes to these behaviors. If the partners want to be understandable to each other, they have to integrate the meanings, which their respective partner attributes to her or his own behavior, into the meanings which they themselves attribute to the other's behavior.

Always it remains within the realm of each partner's responsibility to *convey* to the other, which meanings s/he ascribes to her or his own behavior. It is the respective other's responsibility to be *interested* in the meanings the partner attributes to her or his own behavior and to *integrate* them into her or his constructions of the meanings of the partner's behavior. If all of this happens, the scheme of the ongoing interaction has to be enlarged. It then looks like this:

3rd *Scheme of Interaction*

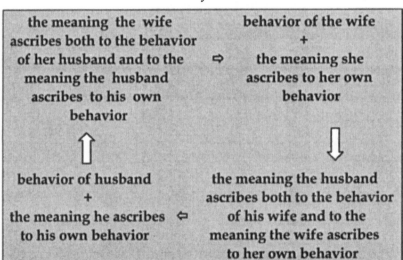

Legend (from top right): The wife interacts by not only behaving but also conveying the meaning that her behavior has for herself. The husband attributes a meaning to the behavior of his wife, which incorporates her own meaning of her behavior. He now behaves and additionally communicates the meaning he ascribes to this behavior. The wife again integrates his meaning into her construction of the meaning she attributes to his behavior.

In many cases, the major part of the therapeutic work with couples consists of supporting the partners to clarify and communicate the meanings, which they attribute both to their own behavior and to the behavior of their respective partner. Ordinarily, many attributions of meanings, both concerning one's own behavior and the partner's behavior, stay out of awareness. Willi et al. (1992) have formalized and described some technical ways of working on this subject during the initial phase of couple therapy. They call their method "constructive differentiation." In my gestalt way of working with couples I usually take a similar direction, but I do not take a previously structured and formalized path. Instead, I relate to the moment-to-moment processes between the partners. Under therapeutic conditions, these processes can be decelerated and looked at in 'slow motion,' so to speak, in order to make more salient what remains invisible under everyday conditions.[11]

In doing so, wife and husband can discover step by step, which emotional meanings their own ways of behavior, as well as those of their respective partner, carry both for themselves and for the other. Thus, they become able to integrate the constructions of their partner into their own respective constructions of their joint situations. Through this mutual exchange, the partners get to know each other's meanings,

> ... and the better they know one another, the more they establish a common representational fund — we speak of *co-representations* ..., which are a precondition of

---

[11] This is what Robert Lee does in his own way when he helps a couple to make explicit what has been "secret language" before.

successful communication. These co-representations ... inform the subject about the ways of behaving, feeling, thinking, and communicating of close interactional partners. (Petzold, 1995, p. 541 – italics in original)

Using Kelly's terminology, one could say that now the stereotypical roles of interaction, about which I have spoken above, are overcome: "To the extent that one person construes the construction processes of another, he may play a role[12] in a social process involving the other person" (1955, p. 73). "Construing the construction processes of another" is nothing else than what Buber called "imagining the real" (1984, p. 286); it is an essential ingredient of every I-Thou relationship between humans (see Staemmler, 1993). Only when this happens, the partner as an autonomous, intentional being in her or his own right becomes real at all. Intersubjectivity occurs—at first in a very basic sense of the word, i.e. the consciousness of the fact that the other—just like oneself—has her or his own thoughts, views, and feelings, which may be in concordance with those of the partner, but may also differ from them. As soon as this kind of intersubjectivity has been established, the marriage has a new chance of growing.

Usually, working on this second subject-matter of couple therapy has a comfortable effect on the partners. Similar to the work on the first subject-matter, the experience of differences

---

[12] In my view Kelly's choice of the word "role" in *this* sentence is very unfortunate: According to his own definition, in role behavior the "social circumstances", i. e. the "construction processes of another", are neglected. I assume that here Kelly used the phrase "to play a role" in the everyday sense.

may be in the foreground, but, most of the time, it is balanced or even superseded by pleasant feelings which arise from being confirmed in one's own right to see the world from one's very private perspective. These feelings are extremely important for some couples, given their background of year- or sometimes decade-long experiences of reciprocal devaluations, invalidations, and neglects of each other's experience. As we all know, "chronic disaffirmation is one of the more insidious tortures to which people can be subjected" (Wile, 1993, p. 83). The end of this torture is a tremendous relief for both partners and the beginning of a fertile dialogue.

Progressions

The partners in my example, now, start to listen to each other and to become interested in what their common situations may look like from the perspective of the respective other. The mutual listening regularly leads to surprises, amazements, and 'aha'-experiences on both sides, once the partner's constructions, which had been ignored for so long, are being realized. Frequently the partners find out that they previously have forced the respective other into unrealistically extreme positions, while occupying the opposite extreme for themselves. The husband becomes aware again that he too has a wish for joint non-sexual activities and for intimacy, and the wife rediscovers her desire for sexual excitement and lust. Sometimes in one or both of them, regretful, guilty, or repentant feelings come up regarding their previous behaviors. If the partners succeed in asking each other's forgiveness and in granting it each to the other, very moving moments of closeness and understanding can occur.

Yet, the differences between the partners' respective experience of their joint situations still exist. For the wife, closeness still precedes sexual approaches, and the husband still tends to induce feelings of closeness through sex. Frequently, however, this difference does not stimulate severe problems anymore, since the process that has taken place between the partners so far provided the wife with the sort of joint non-sexual activities which for her is the precondition of sexual contact. With this precondition given, the partners may find a way out of their vicious circle and to reunite sexually again.

It is my experience that the progress which has been reached until this point rarely is stable. The everyday routine with its many stressful influences as well as the residual differences of the wife's and the husband's meanings are likely to induce some kind of relapse into the old cycle. If the partners can make good use of what has happened in their therapy up to this point, they may be able to relate to each other in a positive way, again, presently, breaking out of the circle, once more. Nevertheless, as before, this balance is also fragile.

A relatively stable balance can only be established, if the couple finds a *common denominator*. Some couples try to find it in agreements, compromises, and arrangements about how they want to deal with conflictual situations. Other methods of adaptation and keeping the common balance may be the voluntary renunciation of the satisfaction of certain needs or at least the willingness to accept a reduction of its frequency.

Concentrating on children, business, and other external activities are favorite methods, too.

As most people know, common denominators like these do not provide a solid long term basis for a relationship. Even when they do, there is a serious disadvantage to them: They reduce the liveliness and the intensity of the relationship. New impulses become rare. The times of destructive fights may be over, but there is also not much excitement between the partners, no new falling in love with each other, no new horizons. Full vitality in a marriage is possible only if the common denominator at the basis of the relationship is not a compromise between the individual and different constructions, but if the common denominator encompasses them and at the same time transcends them.

Joint Constructions

This takes me to the third subject-matter of couple therapy. I see it in the elaboration and/or discovery of joint meanings, which are built upon mutual knowledge of and respect for the individual meanings of the partners and which also integrate them into a system of meanings on a higher, relational level. The following scheme of interaction describes this system formally:

4th Scheme of Interaction

the meaning the wife ascribes both to the behavior of her husband and to the meaning the husband ascribes to his own behavior within the frame of a joint system of meaning ⇨	behavior of the wife + the meaning she ascribes to her own behavior
behavior of husband + the meaning he ascribes to his own behavior ⇦	⇩ the meaning the husband ascribes both to the behavior of his wife and to the meaning the wife ascribes to her own behavior within the frame of of a joint system of meaning

Legend (from top right): The wife interacts by not only behaving but also conveying the meaning that her behavior has for herself. Within the frame of a system of meanings, which has been developed *jointly* by husband and wife, the husband attributes a meaning to the behavior of his wife, which incorporates her own meaning of her behavior. He now behaves and additionally communicates the meaning he ascribes to this behavior. Within the frame of their system of joint meanings, the wife integrates his meaning into her construction of the meaning she attributes to his behavior.

What all of this means in detail can be illustrated by the following example. A possible joint meaning regarding the different individual meanings which a sexual approach has for each partner, could be found in the opinion held by the two partners, that being different is useful and supportive for the maintenance and the development of their marriage. From this joint perspective, being different turns out to be some kind of guarantee that both intimacy *and* sexuality will take place—in which both man *and* woman are interested. The husband will be welcomed by his wife for his greater sensitivity regarding lack of sexual arousal, because he is especially competent in taking care of sexual needs. In reverse, the wife is welcomed by her husband for her greater sensitivity regarding lack of closeness, because she is especially alert to this level of their relationship. Maybe, they will discover:

> The quality of sexual life is intimately related to the quality of mutual holding within a marriage. While a good sexual relationship rests on a secure mutual holding relationship, it also performs a reciprocal function of supporting the holding between marital partners. (Scharff & Scharff, 1991, pp. 25f.).

Within such a joint frame of reference, being different can acquire the meaning of a synergistic fact. This may even make it possible for the partners to find out completely new ways of intimate relating, once sexual excitement and closeness are linked instead of following one another (see Staemmler, 1985). Within this frame the uniqueness of one partner can stay intact and at the same time unite with the uniqueness of the other on a higher level.

> Intimacy between people is achieved when the two urges of self-assertion and mergence striving are in balance with each other. Each person is taking responsibility for defining himself or herself openly in the relationship; each person is also open to discovering the other in his

or her particularity; and in the process of declaring themselves to each other, the partners move toward merging into one unit. (Lichtenberg, 1991, p. 34).

Within the system of joint constructions, the individualities of woman and man remain; they are both the starting points and the future bases of their mutual attraction and enable them to develop a growing system of joint meanings and ways of relating, which goes far beyond the mere knowledge of, and tolerance for, differences.

Now, for the partners a relational dimension opens up which is much more than, and different from, the sum of their individual constructions. From the viewpoint of joint constructions, what had been indicated before by the words "intersubjectivity," "co-representation," or "I-Thou," on one hand proves to be the condition *sine qua non* of the new state of affairs, which could be designated with terms such as "community," "inter-representation," or as simple as — "we." On the other hand, I and Thou do not dissolve as they do within confluent arrangements; instead, they take on a new, secondary rank within the now dominant joint system, into which they are being integrated.[13]

For the partners new priorities result. Now, it is no longer most important for them, to convey their individual needs and interests to each other and to gain space within the relationship for their individual positions. Their first priority becomes what

---

[13] What I call a "joint construction" is therefore both quantitatively and qualitatively more than Petzold's "co-representations."

they need and want from their relationship and how their individual interests can be integrated into their joint system in a way that is meaningful and satisfactory for *both* of them. *Self-realization* of the individual partners is not their primary goal; being-in-relation and the development of their relationship become the predominant values. The self-realization of the two individuals takes second position and becomes a manifestation of their being-in-relation.[14]

To look at it this way is to leave the tenets of Perls's "gestalt prayer" behind. In his alternative "gestalt prayer," Tubbs (1972) poetically expresses much of what I have been formulating:

> If I just do my thing and you do yours,
> We stand in danger of losing each other
> And ourselves.
>
> I am not in this world to live up to your expectations;
> But I am in this world to confirm you
> As a unique human being,
> And to be confirmed by you.
>
> We are fully ourselves only in relation to each other;
> The I detached from a Thou
> Disintegrates.

---

[14] Lynne Jacobs draws on Buber and assumes, that such a relation between self-realization and being-in-relation already exists on an anthropological level: "People do not seek relatedness *to* maintain a self structure, but rather, *self-realization is an occurrence of relatedness*" (1995, p. 155, italics in original). In this view, the joint constructions described above can be interpreted as realizations of this anthropological condition.

I do not find you by chance;
I find you by an active life
Of reaching out.

Rather than passively letting things happen to me,
I can act intentionally to make them happen.

I must begin with myself, true;
But I must not end with myself:
The truth begins with two.

Tubbs's alternative "gestalt prayer" does not completely describe what I call "joint constructions," but it sure points in the same direction. Perhaps somebody who has greater lyrical talents than I might be able to translate my prosaic descriptions into the form of a poem.

Summary

The subject-matter in gestalt therapy with couples, as I see it, is threefold. It consists of:

1. the process of clarification of the respective *responsibilities* of the partners for their own behavior and for their attribution of meanings;
2. the work on the partners' awareness of the fundamental fact that the other views the world and operates from her or his own and *independent* system of constructions; this includes a mutual informing the other partner of one's own meanings, as well as an interest in the partner's meanings; and
3. the elaboration and/or discovery of joint meanings, which are built upon mutual knowledge of, and respect

for, the individual meanings of the partners and which also integrate them into a system of meanings on a higher, relational level.

On a more abstract level, the subject-matter of couple therapy could be characterized as support for a process of change regarding the partners' *interaction*. This support aims at the development of an increasingly complex system of representational constructions, on which the partners found their interaction. Depending on which of the schemes of interaction given above the partners' interaction follows, therapeutic support is provided to facilitate or to make possible an interaction, which is described by the next more complex scheme of interaction. Accordingly, the diagnostic task for the couple therapist(s) is to find out which pattern of interaction the couple exhibits at a given point in time.

In a certain sense the three subject-matters stand in a hierarchical order, since each of them builds upon and presupposes the preceding one. This can easily be derived from the fact, that the respective schemes of interaction become more and more complex. I do not intend to give the impression, however, that they are related to strictly sequential phases of the therapy process. In the course of couple therapy, all of the three subject-matters come into the foreground again and again. Nevertheless, in most cases, at the beginning of couple therapy, the question of the responsibilities absorbs a greater amount of time than it does at a later period. With some couples, a large number of sessions has to be devoted to this question, especially if they are heavily entangled in blaming each other.

In the final stage of couple therapy, the development of joint systems of meanings normally demands more time, but that is not to say that this subject-matter would show up only then. Most couples bring with them some more or less elaborated systems of joint constructions, when they come to therapy in the first place. In a more general sense, even the mutual agreement of the partners on the stimulus-response model of interaction can be interpreted as a system, which the partners construct and maintain jointly—mostly unawares and in spite of the many frustrations it causes.

In conclusion, the three subject-matters cannot be separated distinctly. In practice, they are interwoven with each other and, during the entire course of couple therapy, deserve the attention of both clients and therapists, again and again. However, the co-construction of joint meanings is the ultimate goal and a necessary condition for a shared language of intimacy.

References

Bergner, R. M., & Bergner, L. L. (1990). Sexual misunderstanding: A descriptive and pragmatic formulation. *Psychotherapy 27(3)*, 464-467.

Buber, M. (1965). *The Knowledge of Man: A Philosophy of the Interhuman*. New York: Harper Torchbooks.

Buber, M. (1984). *Das Dialogische Prinzip*. Heidelberg: Lambert Schneider.

Gehrke, S., & Moxom, J. (1962). Diagnostic classifications and treatment techniques in marriage counseling. *Family Process 1*, 253-264.

Goethe, J. W. v. (1976). Maximen und Reflexionen. Frankfurt/M.: Insel.

Gray, J. (1992). *Men are from Mars, Women are from Venus: A Practical Guide for Improving Communication and Getting What You Want in Your Relationships*. New York: HarperCollins.

Greenberg, L. S., & Johnson, S. M. (1988). *Emotionally Focused Therapy for Couples*. New York: Guilford.

Harman, R. L. (1989). *Gestalt Therapy with Groups, Couples, Sexually Disfunctional Men, and Dreams*. Springfield, IL: Charles C. Thomas.

Jacobs, L. (1995). Self psychology, intersubjectivity theory, and gestalt therapy: A dialogic perspective. In R. Hycner & L. Jacobs, *The Healing Relationship in Gestalt Therapy: A Dialogic/Self Psychology Approach* (pp. 129-158). Highland, NY: Gestalt Journal Press.

Kelly, G. A. (1955). *The Psychology of Personal Constructs—Vol. I: A Theory of Personality, Vol. II: Clinical Diagnosis and Psychotherapy*. New York: Norton.

Lakoff, J., & Johnson, M. (1980). *Metaphors We Live By*. Chicago, IL: University of Chicago Press.

Lichtenberg, P. (1991). Intimacy as a function of autonomy and merging. *The Gestalt Journal 14(1)*, 27-43.

Maturana, H. R., & Varela, F. J. (1987). *The Tree of Knowledge: The Biological Roots of Human Understanding*. Boston & London: Shambala.

McWirther, N. (1992, January 20). He needs sex for intimacy; she needs intimacy for sex. *Detroit Free Press*.

Mead, G. H. (1934). *Mind, Self and Society*. Chicago, IL: University of Chicago Press.

Perls, F. S. (1973). *The Gestalt Approach & Eye Witness to Therapy*. Palo Alto, CA: Science and Behavior Books.

Petzold, H. G., van Beek, Y., & van der Hoek, A.-M. (1995). Grundlagen und Grundmuster intimer emotionaler Kommunikation und Interaktion, Intuitive Parenting und Sensitive Caregiving von der Säuglingszeit über die Lebensspanne. In. H. G. Petzold (Hg.), *Psychotherapie und Babyforschung—Vol. II, Die Kraft Liebevoller Blicke —Säuglin Sbeobachtungen Revolutionieren die Psychotherapie* (pp. 491-645). Paderborn: Junfermann.

Richards, J., & von Glaserfeld, E. (1987). Die Kontrolle der Wahrnehmung und die Konstruktion von Realität— Erkenntnistheoretische Aspekte des Rückkoppelungs-Kontroll-Systems. In S. J. Schmidt (Hg.), *Der Diskurs des Radikalen Konstruktivismus* (pp. 192-228). Frankfurt/M.: Suhrkamp.

Sameroff, A. J., & Emde, R. N. (Eds.) (1989). *Relationship Disturbances in Early Childhood: A Developmental Approach.* New York: Basic Books.

Scharff, D. E., & Scharff, J. S. (1991). *Object Relations Couple Therapy.* Northvale, NJ: Jason Aronson.

Sroufe, L. A. (1989). Relationships and relationship disturbances. In A. J. Sameroff & R. N. Emde (Eds.): *Relationship Disturbances in Early Childhood: A Developmental Approach* (pp. 97-124). New York: Basic Books.

Staemmler, F.-M. (1985). Arbeit und Mut—Über Sexualität, Kontakt und Nähe. *Gestalt-Publikationen 1* (Zentrum für Gestalttherapie, Würzburg).

Staemmler, F.-M. (1993). *Therapeutische Beziehung und Diagnose— Gestalttherapeutische Antworten.* München: Pfeiffer.

Staemmler, F.-M. (1997). Towards a theory of regressive processes in gestalt therapy: On time perspective, developmental model and the wish to be understood. *The Gestalt Journal 20(1),* 49-120.

Stern, D. N. (1989). The representation of relational patterns: Developmental considerations. In: A. J. Sameroff & R. N. Emde, (Eds.) (1989): *Relationship Disturbances in Early Childhood: A Developmental Approach* (pp. 52-69). New York: Basic Books.

Tubbs, W. (1972). Beyond Perls. *Journal of Humanistic Psychology 12/2,* 5.

Wardetzki, B. (1991). *Weiblicher Narzißmus—Der Hunger nach Anerkennung.* München: Kösel.

Watzlawick, P., Beavin, J. H., & Jackson, D. D. (1969). *Menschliche Kommunikation—Formen, Störungen, Paradoxien.* Bern: Hans Huber.

Wheeler, G. (2000). *Beyond Individualism: Toward a New Understanding of Self, Relationship, and Experience.* Hillsdale, NJ: Analytic Press (Gestalt Press).

Wile, D. B. (1993). *Couples Therapy: A Nontraditional Approach.* New York: John Wiley & Sons.

Willi, J., Limacher, B., Frei, R., & Brassel-Ammann, L. (1992). Die Technik der Konstruktdifferenzierung in der Paartherapie. *Familiendynamik 17(1),* 68-82.

Zinker, J. C. (1983): Complementarity and the middle ground in couples. *The Gestalt Journal* 6(2), 13-27.

Zinker, J. C. (1992). The gestalt approach to couple therapy. In E. C. Nevis (Ed.), *Gestalt Therapy: Perspectives and Applications* (pp. 285-304). New York: Gardner Press.

Afterword

•••••••••••

As I look back on the journey I have taken in compiling this book, I am revisited by the wonder I experience when sitting with couples. Integral to this way of working with couples is the task of helping couple members *move from an individualistic to a relational sense of the world.* In particular, to move from a sense that they must be alone and isolated in specific, hidden ways (determined by their ground shame) to a sense that they might be received and that a connection is possible.

The process requires a willingness to be affected by the couples we see, to appreciate and affirm their humanity—their experience, pain, hope, yearnings, and the strategies and behavior they have adapted to cope and survive. It means understanding and appreciating them in terms of the fields, as Staemmler says, the meaning systems, in which they have lived—their cultural, ethnic, gender, familial, educational, occupational, economic, and other relevant experience and background.

What we need to look for are the places couple members can and cannot meet—what they do well, what they have difficulty with, and the style with which they do it. Following the signs of shame and belonging allows us to see the couple's system irregardless of topic or content.

For couples to engage in something different than the creative adjustments that they have found to deal with their life lessons of non-reception, from infancy on, requires new experience. And new experience is only possible through sufficient support. Consequently, this way of working with couples is an ongoing adventure in locating necessary support— continually adjusting experiments in order to provide sufficient safety, challenge, relevancy and connection.

Without sufficient support couple members are thrown back on the imperative to hide/camouflage (most often without awareness) there underlying yearnings and their aloneness, including from themselves. This is the power and the purpose, the protective aspect of shame.

However, success with the above brings further complications. As couple members feel safer and they start to have access to their protected yearnings, their shame will be activated, and they will pull them back from acting on these ways of being in the world. As therapists, we must be alert to the inevitability of this response when that which has been kept secret and held as taboo begins to emerge. At these moments further support of the underlying yearnings is crucial.

Helping couples to tolerate the experience of shame (e.g., through compassion, further connection with each other, humor, structure, or education) with or without naming it as such, is of major importance. A first step in this process is helping couple members keep their sense of balance when their partner becomes triggered by shame. Unhooking the power of couple shame cycles in this way is paramount. We must develop an atmosphere in which reception to underlying yearnings is possible, and in which testing this condition is safe, supported and even enticing.

The first person to be triggered by shame in a couple is usually more deeply controlled by this affect and is less likely to be able to take in anything new. In my experience, it is the second couple member that most often possesses the best possibility, with sufficient support, of bearing his/her shame and not perpetuating the couple shame cycle. Sometimes at this point it is possible for the second person to disconnect from the couple's habitually reactive dance and to reach out to his/her partner in some new manner that will connect with his/her partner. However, especially early on, this might mean helping the second couple member to understand that his/her partner is unavailable for the time being, to treat the partner compassionately, and to take care of him/her self until his/her partner emerges from the experience of shame.

Once couple members are able to sufficiently unhook from their couple shame cycles, they will often find themselves in touch with, and wanting to express and act on their underlying yearnings. Yet they may also find that they are in uncharted territory and have little voice or strategy with which to communicate. It is important for the therapist to hear/notice and support the birthing of these emerging voices as the couple experiments with new ways of being with each other.

Underlying this approach is the principle that we are enabling couples to respond, as Spagnuolo Lobb says to restore their spontaneity. Once they are able to creatively meet and hold each other's experience as dearly as they hold their own, they are ready to continue their adventure of living as a couple on their own. This, of course, does not mean that they will be free from the experience of shame, nor from having differences. Instead, it means they will experience their differences in the context of being a team rather than adversarially, and they will be able to use their and their partner's experiences of shame as signs of needed support in their relationship (as the O'Neills say, jointly holding their evolving sense of their individuality and their "oneness").

Working with couples in this way also means understanding that we, as therapists, will occasionally misstep. In such instances we must forgive ourselves and undertake repair with the couple. The value of any intervention, no matter how well thought out or intentioned, must be examined in the light of how the couple responds. We must model the relational perspective that we are helping the couple to embrace by being responsible for helping to locate a place for the couple and us to meet. And we must have enough support in other parts of our lives to be balanced.

This way of working is counter to the idea that is so prevalent in Western culture that a sense of self precedes relationship, which often translates into either greed or isolation. As troubled couples discover the power of their relational connection, something new happens. It is a joy to witness.

January, 2008   Robert G. Lee
                                         Newton, Massachusetts

Appendix

••••••••••

All of the chapters in this book, with one exception, are original manuscripts which were written for this book. The one exception was updated by the author from a previously published article and also contains original material. We are honored that the following three chapters have been published in journals:

A version of Chapter One, "The Secret Language of Intimacy: A Workshop," by Robert G. Lee, appeared in the *International Gestalt Journal*, 2005, 28(1), 93-118.

A version of Chapter Six, "Being at the Contact Boundary with the Other: The Challenge of Every Couple," by Margherita Spanuolo Lobb, appeared in the *British Gestalt Journal*, 2007, 16(1), 44-52.

A version of Chapter Ten, "Joint Constructions: On the Subject Matter of Gestalt Therapy, Exemplified by Gender-Specific Misunderstandings with Regard to Intimacy," by Frank-M. Staemmler appeared in the *Australian Gestalt Journal*, 1997, 1(1), 3-23.

Selected Titles from GestaltPress

An environmentally friendly book printed and bound in England by www.printondemand-worldwide.com

PEFC Certified

This product is
from sustainably
managed forests
and controlled
sources

www.pefc.org

PEFC/16-33-415

Reprint of # - C0 - 229/152/15 - PB - Lamination Gloss - Printed on 03-Oct-18 16:11